Saint Birgitta

Revelations of St. Bridget

on the life and passion of Our Lord, and the life of His Blessed Mother

Saint Birgitta

Revelations of St. Bridget
on the life and passion of Our Lord, and the life of His Blessed Mother

ISBN/EAN: 9783337300050

Printed in Europe, USA, Canada, Australia, Japan

Cover: Foto ©Lupo / pixelio.de

More available books at **www.hansebooks.com**

REVELATIONS OF ST. BRIDGET,

ON THE

LIFE AND PASSION OF OUR LORD,

AND THE

LIFE OF HIS BLESSED MOTHER.

Translated from the Latin.

TO WHICH IS PREFIXED

AN ESSAY ON PRIVATE REVELATIONS, BY REV. WILLIAM H. NELIGAN, D. D.

NEW YORK:
D. & J. SADLIER & CO., 31 BARCLAY-ST.
BOSTON—128 FEDERAL-STREET.
MONTREAL—COR. NOTRE-DAME AND ST. FRANCIS XAVIER STS.
1862.

Entered according to Act of Congress, in the year 1862,

By D. & J. SADLIER & CO.,

In the Clerk's Office of the District Court of the United States for the Southern District of New York.

Preface.

To many of his saints, who meditated so devoutly and so affectionately on his life and passion, our Blessed Lord has been pleased to exhibit them more clearly. Where supported by the recognized sanctity of the individual, and the absence of delusion, the Church has permitted their circulation as useful and edifying, and many have in all ages had a certain weight with the faithful. It is not easy to explain what that weight is, except by saying that the use and influence of these revelations is purely devotional.

Among the revelations of canonized saints and other holy personages, none have exercised a wider influence, or been more frequently cited, than those of St. Bridget; and to make accessible to the English reader, writings of which he has heard from childhood, we have selected from the old Latin folio such as bear on the Life and Passion of our Lord, and the Life of his Blessed Mother, in the hope that it may increase the reader's love for both.

"Nothing is more famous in the life of St. Bridget," says the learned Alban Butler, "than the many revelations with which she was favored by God, chiefly concerning the sufferings of our Blessed Saviour, and revolutions which were to happen in certain kingdoms. It is certain that God, who communicates himself to his servants in many ways, with infinite condescension, and distributes his gifts with infinite wisdom, treated this great saint and certain others with special marks of his goodness, conversing frequently with them in a most familiar manner, as the devout Blosius observes. Sometimes he spoke to them in visions, at other times he discovered to them hidden things by supernatural illustrations of their understanding, or by representations raised in their imaginations so clearly, that they could not be mistaken in them; but to distinguish the operations of the Holy Ghost, and the illusions of the enemy, requires great prudence, and attention to the just criteria or rules for the discernment of spirits. Nor can any private revelations ever be of the same weight and certainty with those that are public, which were made to the prophets, to be by them promulgated to the Church, and confirmed to men by the sanction of miracles and the authority of the Church.

The learned divine, John de Torrecremata, afterwards cardinal, by the order of the council of Basil examined the book of St. Bridget's revelations, and approved it as profitable for the instruction of the faithful; which approbation was admitted by the council as competent and sufficient. It, however, amounts to no more than a declaration that the doctrine contained in that book is conformable to the orthodox faith, and the revelations piously credible upon an historical probability. The learned Cardinal Lambertini, afterwards Pope Benedict XIV., writes upon this subject as follows: "The approbation of such revelations is no more than a permission, that, after a mature examination, they may be published for the profit of the faithful. Though an assent of Catholic faith be not due to them, they deserve a human assent according to the rules of prudence, by which they are probable and piously credible, as the revelations of Blessed Hildegardis, St. Bridget, and St. Catharine of Sienna."

The revelations of St. Bridget, as taken down by her confessors, were printed as early as 1492, and many subsequent editions have appeared. The following translations are made from the Antwerp edition of 1611, and are probably the first in English of any part of her revelations, although the Angelical Discourse, or Office of our Lady, was printed at London, by Caxton, the first English printer.

CONTENTS.

	PAGE
PREFACE	i
ESSAY ON PRIVATE REVELATIONS	vii
I. Prayer of Praise and Thanksgiving, on the Life and Passion of our Lord	9
II. Prayer of Praise and Thanksgiving, on the Life of the Blessed Virgin	15
III. The Immaculate Conception	25
IV. Birth of the Blessed Virgin	26
V. Early Life of the Blessed Virgin	28
VI. The Visitation	32
VII. Her Life with St. Joseph	35
VIII. The Nativity	37
IX. The Purification	41
X. On the Flight into Egypt	44
XI. The Life of Jesus before his Passion	46
XII. Our Lord's appearance	49
XIII. The Baptism of our Lord in the Jordan	50
XIV. The State of the World when Christ began to preach	52
XV. The Agony in the Garden	55
XVI. The Passion of our Lord	57
XVII. The Passion	64
XVIII. The Crucifixion	68

XIX. The Death of our Lord	73
XX. The Burial of our Lord	75
XXI. Our Lady's compassion	77
XXII. The Consideration of the Passion	81
Fruits of the Passion	81
How Sinners Crucify our Lord	83
XXIII. Life of the Blessed Virgin after our Lord's Ascension	84
XXIV. Select Prayers of St. Bridget	87

PRIVATE REVELATIONS:

THEIR AUTHORITY AND THEIR USE.

THE Catholic faith rests upon the revelations made by God to the Apostles and to the Prophets, who have written by inspiration the Holy Scriptures, and who have transmitted to us the dogmas which constitute ecclesiastical tradition. This is the opinion of St. Thomas Aquinas. All theologians agree with him in this, especially Benedict XIV. "Our faith," writes the angelic doctor, "is founded on the revelation made to the apostles and prophets, who have written the canonical books, not on any revelation (if such exist) which may have been made to other teachers." The Catholic faith has passed through eighteen hundred years, without receiving any substantial increase. St. Thomas proposes the following question in the second part of his *Summa Theologica:* "Whether the articles of faith have increased in accordance with the succession of years." He answers it in the following words: "We must say that in so much as the substance of articles of faith is concerned, no addition has been made to it; for whatever is believed in those latter years was contained in the faith of the fathers who preceded us, though it was so in an implicit manner. So far as *explicit* belief is concerned, the number of the articles have increased, as certain matters are known at the present day explicitly, which were not so in former times." The Church has always had belonging to it persons who, endowed with the spirit of prophecy, had received divine revelations, not, however, that they should establish a new faith. St. Thomas maintains this also when he teaches us, that " although there have been at different times in the Church those who were endowed with the spirit of prophecy, they obtained this gift, not to teach a new article of faith, but to direct men in the path of holiness."

Benedict XIV. follows those principles in his work on the " Canonization of Saints." He states that our faith rests, not on the revelation of private persons, but on the public teaching of the prophets and the apostles, and that the succession of ages has not added to the substance of faith.

The only revelation made to the Church is that of the apostles and prophets, which is founded in the divine traditions which the Church preserves and teaches infallibly. No private revelation can ever come from God, if it be opposed to the Holy Scriptures, to divine and apostolic traditions, and to the public definitions of the Church. St. Paul states, in his Epistle to the Galatians (i. 8), " though we, or an angel from heaven, preach a Gospel to you besides that which we have preached to you, let him be anathema."

In his Epistle to the Thessalonians he writes as follows (2 Thess. ii. 14): "Hold the traditions which you have learned, whether by word or our epistle;" and to the Hebrews he gave this admonition (i. 3–9), "Be not carried away with various and strange doctrines." Every private revelation should be rejected as an imposture, and as an illusion of the devil, which is not in conformity with holy writ and the apostolical traditions which the Church has infallibly defined. It does not follow from this, that if these revelations agree with the teaching of the Church, we are to look upon them as coming from heaven. We must arrive at the same conclusion respecting those which contain something contrary to the unanimous teaching of the fathers and theologians; for this unanimous teaching of the fathers cannot err in matters of faith. Therefore the Council of Trent has forbidden the interpreting of Holy Scripture contrary to the unanimous consent of the fathers. It is also of the same effect if theologians teach unanimously that any doctrine is deduced from the principles of the faith. Their unanimity upon matters connected with faith and morals supplies so valid an argument, that no person can oppose it without being a heretic, or at least without coming very near to heresy; for any teaching contrary to the unanimous consent of the fathers or theologians is heretical, or borders on heresy. The fathers are said to be unanimous when the most eminent in all parts of the world agree in teaching the same truth, without any of those who have been always considered as orthodox disagreeing from it.

A question arises as to what we are to think of private revelations which have opposed to them the general opinion of theologians, and of those which say that matters which are freely debated in the schools have been made known to them as certain; and of those which allege new doctrines, or which before were not known. Many authors of great weight think that such revelations should be rejected; for the object of a revelation from God should be in perfect conformity with the rule of faith, which teaches that the point spoken of is only one of opinion in the Church. If, for instance, any person said he had revelation respecting grace physically, determining the will to good as the Thomists teach, we would see in this the private opinion of the man, and not a supernatural revelation. Others assert the possibility of private revelations on questions which are not yet decided by the Church. They say that we have no right to place limits to the power of God, and maintain that he cannot make a revelation respecting a controverted question. The schools of the Thomists and Scotists have differed on the following question: "If Adam had not sinned, would Christ have come into the world in consequence of the decree of God?" We cannot doubt the possibility of a revelation on this point. The holy see has given its approbation to revelations upon matters of mere opinion, in the schools. This shows that revelations should not be rejected, although the approbation of them does not take the matters to which they refer from that of opinions where they have been placed by the controversies of the schools. To maintain that revelations on controversies which the Church has not decided are not to be rejected, by no means goes to prove that these revelations have decided the questions, or that the controversies respecting them have ceased. Some writers hold that the revelations which appear to be contrary to the general teaching of theologians, should be examined with more attention than others. Benedict XIV. quotes on this subject *Martin del Rio*, who says: "If any thing is repugnant to the more usual opinion of the scholastics, it is not to be at once condemned as erroneous, if, when piously and prudently understood, it is proved by its own approved authors, and by reasons which are not absurd." Hustado makes the supposition of a revelation being contrary to the common opinion of the fathers and theologians, and concludes that it is not on that account to be rejected as diabolical, but demands greater attention and a more careful examination. The result of what has been stated seems to be, that if the teaching of the fathers and theologians be morally unanimous, and a private revelation proposes something contrary to this, it is to be rejected as devoid of any authority. This seems to be the opinion of all writers. If it be not in conformity with the general decision of the fathers and the theologians, several authors look upon it as apocryphal; others regret all revelations which are connected with what are mere matters of opinion in the Church, as not being in accordance with the rule of faith. On these two latter points writers differ. It will, therefore, be necessary to inquire what influence private revelations should have on matters where opinions respecting them are free.

There are some revelations recorded respecting matters which the Church and tradition have spoken nothing about; as, for instance, some mystery or circumstance connected with the life and passion of our Saviour and the Blessed Virgin, which is not to be met with either in Scripture, tradition, the definitions of the Holy See, or the writings of the fathers. Must we reject such revelations as apocryphal? Suarez makes the following judicious observations: "In meditating on the passion of our Lord, we must not, at our own pleasure, suppose matters connected with it, which the Evangelists do not mention, or which cannot be deduced from the expositions which the fathers have given respecting it. The faithful can piously meditate on the bitterness of the passion, and on the circumstances connected with it, and excite their sympathies by the circumstances which are related, and judging how these may have happened. It is not proper to invent new matter connected with it, for this cannot be free from temerity, or from the danger of being considered as false." While all theologians admit this doctrine as certain, they do not exclude the possibility of Divine revelations upon those parts of the mysteries which Scripture and tradition pass over in silence. It is on this account that many writers do not reject altogether these revelations. They say that the only revelation to be condemned and to be feared, is that which prescribes a new rule of conduct, which interferes with Christian discipline, or which endangers the salvation of souls. The *thesis* transmitted to the Inquisition of Spain respecting the revelations of the venerable Mary of Agreda, by John Cortez Ossorius, shows that private revelations should not be rejected for this reason. We propose, before we conclude, to show the evidence we are to give to private revelations belonging to the mysteries or the circumstances connected with them. Baronius, in his Annals, makes mention of some revelations which had been made in the fourteenth century, during the Western schism. The English nation had given their adhesion to Urban VI., and were desirous of showing that his cause was better than that of his competitor. They adduced the revelations of a hermit, who said that, when celebrating Mass, he knew by a supernatural manner that Urban VI. was the legitimate pope. No person seemed to pay any credit to him. The answer given to him was as follows: "That no account should be paid to this, for the canons show that we are not to believe these invisible revelations, unless a miracle which can be proved, or the special testimony of Scripture attest it. Otherwise, our faith would be in danger from the false assertion of heretics, who act in a manner similar to this." Another person said he had frequent communications with the heavenly spirits. He lived fifteen years in the desert, and declared to Urban VI. that he was a false Pope. As he could give no proof of his mission, the Pope ordered him to be punished severely, and he confessed his imposture. The French prelates who were with Urban VI. interfered and obtained his pardon. This shows how little faith is to be placed in revelations respecting the public affairs of the Church, when no visible proof of their authenticity can be produced. All useless revelations should be rejected, especially if calculated only to excite curiosity, and if not in conformity with the wisdom and attributes of God. Benedict XIV. places them in the same catalogue with those that are opposed to Scripture, and the tradition of the Church, and considers that they should be regarded as apocryphal. "What has been said," writes the learned Pontiff, "respecting these revelations which are opposed to Scripture, apostolical tradition, the unanimous consent of the fathers and theologians, applies to those in which something bad is recommended; or if good be counselled, it is only as an impediment to a greater good; or if bad and good be mixed together, the same applies if lies and contradictions are found mixed up together; or if useless or curious things be mentioned in them, a like conclusion may be come to—if the revelation could be known by human reason, or if, though the matter does not exceed the power of God, it is not in conformity with the wisdom of God and his attributes." The proper mark of the agency of Satan is to have no utility connected with them. The revelations of useless or merely curious matters, is either the result of imposture or of infernal spirits. Divine revelation serves the purpose of instructing Christians.

The Centuriators of Magdeburg are opposed to all revelations which are not contained in the canonical books. Melancthon ranges all such among superstitions and fables. While others admit some Divine revelations, besides those contained in the canon of Scripture, they refuse their assent to those, which some holy women have had, not believing that they are inspirations of the Holy Ghost. No good Catholic will join in their opinion. Gravina traces the rules by which we can know true from false revelations. He shows, that in the first place we must admit many private revelations, the proofs of which are recorded in the history of the Church. Secondly, That heretics have endeavored to get rid of revelations which are really from God. Thirdly, That a multitude of impostors have tried to gain credit for false revelations. Fourthly, That the gift of revelations exists even now in the Church. In proof of this, the revelations of St. Hildegarde, St. Litgarde, St. Angela of Bohemia, St. Bridget, St. Theresa, and many other saints, are quoted as deserving the approbation of the Church. The approbation which the Church has given to many of them, is a sufficient answer for the Catholic to the objection of those who differ from him. The non-cessation of prophecy is not less certain than that of revelation. The Church is very slow in giving her approbation to any revelations, vision, or apparition. The miracle of an immediate cure effected after an apparition of a servant of God, whose intercession is alleged as the cause of it, is often presented for consideration to the Congregation of Rites. If the necessary proofs be forthcoming, approbation will be granted to the miracle, but not to the apparition or the revelation. The Holy See sometimes approves of a vision or an apparition of angels, of the Blessed Virgin, or of our Lord, made to a servant of God, or of a prophecy, or some wonderful prediction. The instances are indeed very rare where it grants the same privilege to a volume of visions, apparitions, or prophecies. This approbation by no means marks them with the certitude of faith. Benedict XIV. writes, "So far as the instances before us warrant us to come to a conclusion, this approbation by no means requires the certitude of faith, but only causes them to be looked upon as probable." It seems that the effect of the approbation of the Holy See is only to give a mere probability to private revelation, and to testify that there is nothing in them contrary to faith or the unanimous teachings of the fathers and theologians. It does not give them certainty, nor demand the assent of the faithful. Cardinal Bonca is of this opinion; he states, "Those revelations which are written by holy men and women are not to be considered as approved, in order that we may assent to them with the certitude of faith, but that we may receive them as probable." The only persons obliged to believe them as supernatural, are those to whom they are made, when they certainly know that they come from God. Others receive them as probable, and in this light the Church proposes them. Her approbation excludes the danger of their being opposed to faith or public teaching, and of their containing any thing contrary to Scripture and tradition—the Church, recognizing them as probable, permits their being published for the benefit of the faithful, as they are calculated to foster piety. The approbation confines itself to this, and adds no more credibility to them.

Theologians divide the approbation which the Holy See gives to a doctrine into three different classes. They call the first definitive, when the Pope declares a doctrine as certain, and which must be followed by all. If any person holds an opinion contrary to this, he is in opposition to the Holy See. The second division which they make is named elective, when it is commended and praised by the Church as one that may be held safely in practice, without condemning those who follow the contrary opinions. The third is styled permissive. In this latter case the Church only says it is free from censure, and states nothing positive respecting it, and does not even commend it. In this last division we may place the approbation which the Church gives to private revelations; for it is simply a permission to have them published for the use of the faithful. In this light Eugenius III. approved of the revelations of St. Hildegarde; Boniface IX. those of St. Bridget; Gregory XI. those of St. Catherine of Sienna. "It should be known," writes Benedict XIV., "that this approbation is nothing more than permission granted, after a careful examination, to have them published for the instruction and use of the faithful." This shows the degree of credence we are to give to revelations which are even approved of. No person can consider them as articles of faith. Theologians teach that we are not allowed to give them the same assent that we give to articles of faith, for they do not possess the divine testimony which is the formal object of faith. A private revelation rests only on the testimony of him who states that he has received it. It resolves itself into human testimony; and the assent which we give it cannot be more than of the same class, and therefore human. The most authentic and the most certain revelation cannot demand that others should give it that assent which they give to what is of divine faith. God may have spoken to him who is the subject of the divine revelation; others can only believe this on his testimony, which cannot be for them the testimony of God. The Church cannot change the essential rules of faith by the approbation which it gives to private revelations. It follows from this that they are incapable of attaining the certitude which divine faith requires from us. "As far as those are concerned," writes Benedict XIV., "to whom the revelation is not made, both Cardinal Luigo and Aranxo maintain that they are not bound to believe those revelations. If they believe them, their assent cannot be such as they give to the Catholic faith, since it is not based on divine testimony, which is the formal and proper ratio of divine faith; it is not resolved proximately into the revelation made to the particular person. The only evidence it possesses is the narration of the person who records it. It cannot be resolved into what is called mediate revelation, since it is not addressed to them, nor does God speak with them. It is resolved, therefore, into the human testimony of him who relates his private revelation to others. Where the formal object of divine faith is wanting, the assent must be mere human faith." Private revelations which are approved of by the Holy See cannot produce certitude; they only give a simple probability to those matters comprised in them. Theologians differ respecting the amount of this probability; all agree that they are to be regarded as merely probable things. When the learned Cardinal Turrecremata approved of the revelations of St. Bridget, he limited himself to the recommending of them as pious, and that they might be read by the faithful without fear of superstition. The following is the form in which he expressed this approbation: "I have examined nearly all the books of the revelations of St. Bridget as accurately as I am able, and none of them, when piously or modestly understood, is contrary to holy writ or the opinions of the fathers. They can be read in the Church, in the same manner as the books of other writers and the history and legends of the saints are permitted to be read." The learned cardinal is careful in attributing any dogmatic value to the revelations which he approves of. "It is of little matter," says Melchior Cano, "whether one believes or not the revelations of St. Bridget or of St. Catherine, for these do not belong to the faith in any respect." Some theologians grant a certain value to private revelations, as making the opinions to which they refer capable of being maintained. They allow that the opinions contrary to them maintain their probability. As an instance of this we may cite the example of Cardinal Turrecremata, who, though he approved of the revelations of St. Bridget, yet he held opinions diametrically opposed to those stated in those revelations. That the opinions held in the schools are yet probable, notwithstanding that private revelations contrary to them have been approved of by the Church, was discussed with much spirit in the writings which the theologians published at Rome in 1730, respecting the cause of Mary of Agreda. "Theologians and mystics confess," they write, "that private revelations, approved of and received (though they must be believed) by those to whom they are made, do not make the opinions contrary to them lose that probability which they had before the revelations. According to some theologians, a private revelation confers a greater probability on the point to which it refers, than the contrary one to it possesses. This is the opinion of Cajitan, who teaches that we ought to receive the Catholic revelations which are made to the apostles and prophets as being those on which our faith is founded, and that we should adhere to private revelations as being more probable. Martin del Rio goes much farther, and seems to think that we should see in them a moral certitude. He writes against Henry Hesse and Sibyllanus, who refused to receive the revelations of St. Bridget and others as undoubtedly true, and as not being dictated by the Holy Ghost. "If this," writes Martin del Rio, "be understood of the certitude of the Catholic faith and its truths, and of all that has been published by the inspiration of the Holy Ghost, it is no doubt true. No person of any weight ever held such an opinion respecting private revelations. We only give to them a moral certitude, or what we attach to human affairs." Such is the opinion of Martin del Rio.

From what has been already stated, it will appear evident that we cannot assent to his views, but must conclude that the only light we can receive private revelations in is, that when the Church grants her approbation to them, we must consider them as such as may be read by the faithful with advantage and profit, like any other book which contains in it nothing contrary to faith or morals.

There are three principles which all theologians acknowledge respecting private revelations: First, that private revelations, although probably certain, authentic, and approved of by the Church, can never be received as Catholic truths, which must be believed as articles of divine faith. The second principle is, that any person is free to believe them or not, provided it is done with modesty, for some good reason, and not through a desire of despising them. Benedict XIV. observes in his work on the Canonization of the Saints, "Any person can hold the Catholic faith safe and entire, and yet not afford an assent to these revelations, provided he does it with a becoming modesty—not without his having a reason for doing so, and without contempt for them." Thirdly, it is possible that apocryphal matters may be found in revelations which have been approved of. Benedict XIV. puts the following question: "Can any thing apocryphal be met with in revelations which have been approved of?" With respect to revelations that have not been approved of, there is no doubt of it. He replies to the question as follows: "With respect to those that have been approved of, we answer in the affirmative." The revelation of St. Michael and St. Elizabeth to St. Bridget has been received as apocryphal, and declared to be such. The saints may have some revelations which have had their origin in their own minds, or in their own preconceived ideas, and not in the supernatural work of the Holy Ghost. The prophets have sometimes stated things which have had their origin in their own minds, though they believed that they came from God; so also it may have been with the saints.

"It may happen," writes Benedict XIV., "that some saint, through his preconceived opinions, or from ideas fixed in his mind, may suppose that certain things were revealed to him by God, when they were really not so." It will be asked, if such be the case, will not an uncertainty like this prevent the Church giving her approbation to private revelations? Gerson answers the question in the following manner: "In the same manner as it is of little importance that certain things which are false be more probable than those which are true, so it is of but little importance that certain things be piously believed. We are not to conclude from this, that we can believe in things when we know them to be false, but that pious credulity does not connect itself with truth or falsehood, but only with the appearance or probability. There is no danger here, for we refer to the appearance or probability. The truth or the falseness of them are equally unknown." St. Jerome observes very wisely that in matters of this description it is better to doubt piously than to define rashly, as each contradictory is probable, and one subsists with the other, not as verity but in probability; under different relations we may believe either one or the other without touching the faith, provided that the mind guards itself from making any absolute assertion. This we state in connection with the miracles and legends of the saints, the lives of the fathers, the visions of devoted persons, the opinions of holy doctors. The Church receives these; she does not require us to believe them in order that we may be saved, but in order that they may serve to excite pious affections in the faithful, and to give them edification. We cannot know with certainty that they are true, nor can we know with certainty that they are false. Therefore the Church does not require us to believe them as necessary. Gravina examines another question connected with private revelations. He inquires if controversies connected with the Catholic faith can be decided by private revelations. He says, in answer to this, that according to some authors, dogmas can be defined not only by Scripture and tradition, but also by other special intimations by which God governs his Church. John Servanus, bishop of Acerno, is mentioned by him as holding this opinion. He enumerates eight other writers who think with him. He, however, agrees with St. Thomas in concluding that our faith rests on the revelations of the apostles and the prophets. This comprises the Word written and the Word not written, and not private revelations. He quotes the following texts (1 Cor. iii. 11), "For no one can lay another foundation but that which is laid; which is Christ Jesus;" also (Hebrews v. 6), "not laying again the foundation."

From these, he concludes that the formal reason of faith rests on the revelation made to the apostles and prophets as the public ministers and official preachers of the Gospel. This excludes altogether new revelations. Our Saviour told his disciples (John xv. 15), "All things whatsoever I heard from my Father, I have made known to you." This proves that he revealed every thing to his apostles. The faith consists in what the Church has received from the apostles. The apostles received it from Christ; Christ received it from his Father. The Church expects no new revelations; it is the Jews who are looking for them. The Church does not wait for new oracles to decide controversies by them; the Word of God, contained in Scripture and tradition, is sufficient for her. St. Paul, in his Epistle to the Galatians, anathematizes an angel, should he preach a Gospel different from what the apostles proclaim. To preach any Gospel besides what has been received, is to teach what the Author of faith has not revealed, and what the public ministers whom He has chosen have not announced. The divine seed which is spoken of in the parable, has been sown by the preaching of the apostles. The children cannot change the seed, nor sow new seed. "It is not fitting," writes Vincent of Lerins, "that any thing should be changed in the nature of the seed; it is rather more necessary that what has been sown by the fathers, should be cultivated through the industry of the children." A new revelation would be the sowing of new seed in the public faith of the Church. The practice of the Church excludes the necessity of private revelations. The Church has not recourse to oracles, when there is need of deciding controversies. She relies on the promises of Christ, who is with her until the consummation of ages. She is certain of the assistance of the Holy Ghost, who teaches her all truth. She explains the Scriptures; she gathers the traditions when she consults the teachings of the fathers and the decisions of Councils. In this manner she decides the controversies of faith. When the question respecting the ceremonies of the law were discussed, St. Peter did not recur to an immediate revelation, but we are told "there was much disputing." After the apostles had examined the matter, they thus conclude: "It hath seemed good to the Holy Ghost and to us." Without any immediate revelation, and with the assistance of the Holy Ghost, they decide on the matter that was disputed among them.

The words of our Lord in Matt. xi., "The prophets and the law prophesied until John," do not mean that the Church has lost the gift of prophecy. They rather signify that the prophets, who foretold the coming of Christ, and the establishing of his kingdom, ceased in John the Baptist, who commenced to preach respecting the kingdom of Heaven, and pointed out our Saviour as he drew near to him. The Church ought to have her prophets. In the Acts of the Apostles we find mention made of them in several places. In the eleventh chapter we have the prediction of Agabus respecting the famine which took place under the Emperor Claudius. In the twenty-first chapter the same prophet announces to St. Paul the persecution which awaited him at Jerusalem. St. John received the revelation of the Apocalypse in the island of Patmos. The precursor of our Lord was the last of the series of prophets who preceded the Messias. The Church was also to have her prophets, who would declare future events, by the revelation of the Holy Ghost. St. Catherine of Bologna uttered a remarkable prediction respecting the taking of Constantinople by Mahomet II. The event justified the prophecy. Its authenticity was proved when the saint was canonized. The imperial city yielded after a siege of two months. It was taken on the eve of Pentecost. God wished to show the world that he punished the Greeks, for the blasphemies which they had uttered against the Holy Ghost. The naval victory at Lepanto was also foretold by Pius V. The holy Pontiff knew by a revelation the day and the hour of the victory. He announced it to several persons who were with him. It was found afterwards that the battle was gained at the very time which the Pontiff had indicated. St. Bernard delivered many prophecies with respect to the crusade which he had preached. Louis, king of France, communicated his project respecting it to many nobles. They were unanimous in their desire to consult the holy abbot of Clairvaux. He referred them to Pope Eugenius III., who approved of the crusade, and authorized St. Bernard to preach it. When the voice of the saint, whom Germany and France honored as a prophet and an apostle, was heard, thousands of men took up the cross. Germany, France, England, and Hungary, joined in the good work. The preaching of St. Bernard was confirmed by innumerable miracles. The monk Ganfridus, his historian, gives the following account respecting it: "He preached with the visible assistance of God, who confirmed his words by the miracles which accompanied them." These were so many and so striking that it would be very difficult to give an account of them, or even to enumerate them. A person begins to describe them, but they soon exceed his powers of writing. Twenty persons, and sometimes more, were cured of their various diseases in the same day. A day was seldom passed without similar prodigies. Our Lord, by bringing persons to touch his servant, opened the eyes of those who were born blind, made the lame to walk, the deaf to hear, and the dumb to speak. Grace restored by a miracle what Nature had left imperfect. These numerous and striking miracles seemed to confirm the predictions of St. Bernard respecting the success of the expedition. The routing of the united armies, and the victories gained over them by the enemy, caused the greatest consternation through the Christian world. St. Bernard, who had been an object of universal veneration, was now treated as a false prophet and an impostor. The revelations of the saint were undoubtedly true. The prophecies which he uttered came really from God. It happens sometimes that true prophets do not know all that the Holy Ghost intends by their visions, their words, and their actions. It is possible that a revelation is true, and comes from God; and that the person who receives it may understand it in a sense different from what God intended it, and give a false explanation of it. The crusaders, who set out for the Holy Land, had their thoughts fixed on the things of earth rather than on those of heaven. Their minds were filled with politics, and not with religion. Their vows brought them to a land where they looked for riches, glory, or the establishment of the kingdom of Jerusalem. What God had in view was the eternal salvation of those who would die for the faith and the Church in this expedition. It was the venerable abbot of Cassamere who discovered this mystery. "It has been told me," he writes, "that you are very sad respecting the expedition to Jerusalem, as it has not turned out as prosperous as you might wish. You are afflicted because the Church of God has not received the increase you desired. God had more in this event than merely to deliver the East from the tyranny of the Pagans. He desired to work the spiritual deliverance of the Westerns. Who is to ask him to give a reason for his acting so? Every wise man would weep over those who have returned to their old sins, and have committed greater ones. He cannot lament for the death of those who enjoy now the fruit of their penance, and have given up their souls to Christ purified by many sufferings. Should you doubt what I say, I can assure you that SS. John and Paul, the patrons of our monastery, have often visited us. I have asked them respecting this circumstance. They answered that a multitude of the fallen angels had been replaced by those who had died in that expedition." Ganfridus relates the fact of a wonderful miracle having been performed by St. Bernard on the very day that he heard of the breaking up of the expedition. The Holy Ghost, which worked through him when he preached the crusade, had not ceased its operations. This miracle, wrought by him at the time when he heard of the sad disaster, caused the world to adore the secret designs of Providence. They no longer charged the saint with the responsibility of an event which happened so contrary to his wishes. It seems, therefore, that a saint who is filled with the Holy Ghost, and who confirms his mission by miracles, may be deceived about the real character of the circumstances respecting which he prophesies. "We should know," says St. Thomas, "that as the pious mind of the prophet is a deficient instrument, as it is called, even true prophets do not know what the Holy Ghost intended by their visions, or words, or facts." "It is not repugnant," writes Benedict XIV., "that a revelation may be true and from God, and that the interpretation given of it by the man may be false, as he understands it differently from what God intended." He relates also the fact connected with St. Bernard, and that the matters did not turn out as he predicted. "We cannot doubt," he writes, " respecting the truth of the revelation and the prophecy; but the divine truth, which is unchangeable, was not understood by the man, and the counsels of man and of God were different."

It seems that when a true prophet does not understand matters according to the mind of God, the events do not agree with his predictions.

No prophet has the gift of prophecy, as an habitual thing. The saints, though enlightened by the Holy Ghost, may deceive themselves, and believe that they have revelations, when these merely arise from their preconceived ideas. A true prophet may, on some occasions, declare things which will not take place, when he speaks of things without a divine revelation. "It may come to pass," writes Benedict XIV., "that those things which are predicted by a true prophet will not come to pass, because, although he supposed he foretold them from a divine inspiration, they were only the thoughts of his own mind." This seems to be the explanation of the mistake into which the saints sometimes fall. God enlightens the prophets in a twofold manner—by an express revelation, and by a secret instinct which their minds receive without their knowing it. The prophets know with the greatest certainty all that is revealed to them. They do not know with the same certainty what comes through their instinct. They cannot discern when it is a divine instinct that animates them, or when they speak what their own mind suggests. All they know by a supernatural instinct is not manifested to them by a prophetic evidence. The predictions which arise from this secret instinct are subject to error. The events turn out the opposite of what they intended.

Prophecies of the saints which are of a threatening character, are often not fulfilled when the condition on which they were uttered ceases to exist. They are not absolute, but are subordinate to these conditions. When the divine justice proclaims punishments, it presupposes the existence of crimes and disorders which need the punishment denounced by the prophet to cause the cessation of them. Should these evils not continue, the prediction will not receive its accomplishment. With respect to the predictions of saints, it should be remarked, that they are expressed sometimes in a doubtful sense, and speak of the future in such a manner as shows that it cannot be a supernatural revelation. This cannot be looked upon as a regular prophecy; it must be considered as a mere conjecture founded on human probabilities. The saint is sometimes under the influence of a particular affection or of a preconceived opinion. At other times he will speak with a trouble of mind, or he may know, through natural means some part of the things which he announces. These circumstances must be taken into account to judge accurately of the nature of these prophecies. "We must see," writes Benedict XIV., "if the person who utters these predictions can, from signs, conjectures, and experience, have any knowledge of those things which he predicts; also if he have revealed the future in a doubtful manner, or if he has made use of the kind of reasoning usually adopted by a person in confirmation of what he has stated. It should also be considered, if he has allowed the hope of temporal reward to affect him, or if he has spoken when his mind was in a state of perturbation, or if he did not know all, or at least some portion, of those things respecting which he has prophesied. All these matters must be carefully inquired into.

We would not include in these observations the predictions of those saints whose gift of prophecy has been approved of as certain, and whose sanctity is acknowledged. There are four cases in which the events do not correspond with the predictions: *First*, When the prophet does not understand things in accordance with the mind of God. *Second*, When he is mistaken in believing he has a private revelation when he is obeying his own private instinct. *Third*, When the prophecies are of a threatening nature. *Fourth*, When they are founded on conjectures, which enables a person to know the nature of the events which he predicts. St. Gregory the Great, in commenting on Ezekiel, remarks that true prophets, in consequence of the frequent habit they have in uttering prophecies, can foretell certain things which are merely the products of their own minds, and yet believe that these come from the spirit of prophecy. He adds, that there is this difference between the true and false prophets. That the former correct the error which they have made, as soon as they become conscious of it; whereas false prophets always persist in their mistake, even after they have become aware of it. The prophet Nathan approved at first the intention which David had of building the temple, and assured him it was God who put the design in his heart. But God ordered the prophet the very same night to go and tell David that this undertaking was reserved for his successor.

Another subject connected with this, presents itself to our notice. If the Church can beatify or canonize a servant of God, whose life does not show any of those extraordinary graces which theologians call *gratis datæ*, in contradistinction to those which are styled *gratum facientes*—should she inquire into the extraordinary graces, before pronouncing on the heroism of the virtues? What are the proper marks whereby we may discover the authenticity of revelations and prophecies? Do these extraordinary graces, when proved to be true and authentic, show a higher degree of sanctity?

A servant of God may have all the Christian's virtues. He practises these to a degree of heroism. He has no extraordinary graces. He foretells events. He has not the gift of tongues or of interpretation. He has no ecstasies or supernatural revelations. In this state of the cause, can the virtues of the holy man be submitted to examination? Can they afterwards examine the miracles which have taken place since his death, and then proceed to beatification and canonization? Is it necessary that in the absence of gratuitous graces they should suspend the judgment referring to the virtues, and stop the cause. Revelations, prophecies, ecstasies, and graces of this class are not necessary in causes of canonization. "The question which is proposed," writes Benedict XIV., "is not said to be defined. If my opinion respecting it should be asked, I should reply that they may safely proceed in the cause of canonization. They can discuss the miracles which have taken place since his death. From what has been said in another part of this work, it appears that only two miracles are required in each cause of canonization and beatification." Two different kinds of proof support this opinion of the learned Pontiff. These are the texts of the canon law, with the interpretation of the doctors and the practice of the Church. The chapter of the Decretals (*Venerabili* 52 *de testibus*) mentions only the life and the miracles of the saint. " We submit to your prudence," writes Honorius III., " the examination of each of the witnesses, whom the abbot and monks of St. Martin will produce, respecting the life and the miracles of the aforesaid abbot N. of pious memory." The Bulls which Gregory IX. published respecting St. Dominic and St. Francis of Assisium show that the sanctity of the life and the miracles form the only object of juridical inquiry in causes of canonization. The same Pontiff canonized St. Anthony of Padua. He says in the Bull of canonization, " Although final perseverance is sufficient, that any person should be accounted a saint in the Church of God—according to what is written, 'To him that overcometh I will give the hidden manna,'—in order that one be considered a saint before men in the Church of God, two things are required, viz., merits and miracles. These render a mutual witness to each other. Neither merits without miracles, nor miracles without merits, are sufficient to prove fully the sanctity of the saint before men. When merits which cannot be found fault with precede, and miracles which are evident follow after, we have a certain proof of the sanctity of the saint. These cause us to venerate him whom God presents to us as venerable both by merits which go before and miracles which follow after." The commentators on the Decretals say that sanctity of life and miracles form the subjects which must be inquired into in all causes of canonization. In all the juridical acts connected with the canonization of saints, we find no traces of gratuitous graces. This description of graces is conferred on sinners as well as saints. They are not conferred on all saints. The utility of the Church does not require that they should have all the special graces which serve the general good. "These," writes St. Augustine, "are not conferred on all the saints, in order that those who suppose themselves ill would be deceived by a most pernicious error, and suppose there were greater gifts than the works of justice, by which eternal life is maintained." Most of the saints have not been gifted with these gratuitous graces; they form no essential condition of their canonization. If these form no essential part in the canonization of a saint, they often impede the progress of the cause. A revelation or a prophecy which is contrary to the faith, to the divine traditions, and to the unanimous teaching of the fathers and theologians, condemns the cause to eternal silence. It is impossible that this revelation comes from God. True sanctity finds in it that which cannot be reconciled with it. Gratuitous graces may be examined in different points of view. The first thing we are bound to see is, if there is any thing contrary to faith and the common teaching of the Church. According to the decrees of Pope Urban VIII., the Congregation of Rites must pass judgment on this before they proceed to examine the virtues. Benedict XIV. teaches as follows: "There must be an examination of the aforesaid revelations. The sacred Congregation must declare that there is nothing in them contrary to faith or morals, and that they teach no new doctrine, or what is different from the common sense or teaching of the Church. Their prophecies are also subject to examination. It must be seen whether they are in conformity with truth and Christian piety. If they are not, though the prediction be a most striking one, and justified by the event to which it refers, it will not prove him to be a true prophet. It will furnish grave doubts respecting the sanctity, and will weaken the other proofs which are offered respecting the virtues. Visions, ecstasies, and other extraordinary graces must be submitted to a similar judgment. Revelations should be suspected when they treat of useless matter and objects calculated to excite curiosity, or when they teach a new doctrine, or present as a revelation any matter which is yet undecided by the tribunal of the Church. If they suggest some unusual matter, the same may also be said respecting them. All revelations of this class are suspicious in their character, and arise from the ideas and preconceived opinions of the servant of God before he had a revelation. These, however, do not impede altogether the cause of beatification. The Congregation proceeds to examine the question—if virtues have been practised to an heroic degree.

If the heroism of the virtues of a person whose cause is before the Congregation of Rites, be not proved legitimately and receive their approbation, neither revelations, prophecies, nor ecstasies will effect much towards his canonization. Supernatural graces, and those of a gratuitous nature, do not of themselves constitute a mark of the sanctity of the person who receives them. It is a question of difficulty to decide whether revelations come from God or not. If it be probable that they do, they will not prove the sanctity of the person, inasmuch as they do not constitute Christian perfection. They do not render a man more pleasing to God, nor more useful to his neighbor. The judgment which is passed in acts of canonization and beatification has for its object to establish the innocence of life and the heroism of the servant of God. These have nothing in common with graces given gratuitously. "We must venerate," writes Gregory the Great in the twentieth book of his Morals, "in good men the humility of charity and not the *eclat* of miracles." For this reason the Church despises the miracles of heretics, because she knows that they are no proof of holiness. Sanctity consists not in performing miracles, but in loving every one as we do ourselves, in believing in God, and in thinking our neighbor better than ourselves. True virtue is charity, and not the working of miracles. St. Jerome, commenting on the Gospel of St. Matthew, writes as follows: "Prophecies, working miracles, driving out devils, do not come from the merit of him who does these works. It is through the invocation of the name of our Lord they are effected. Men, therefore, honor God, who alone works those miracles." What has been said of revelations applies to prophecies. "The grace of prophecy," writes Benedict XIV., "is in its nature a grace gratuitously given." In causes of canonization and beatification, no account will be made of prophecy if it be not preceded by a proof of the heroic virtues. Like the other graces which are given gratuitously, the gift of prophecy is conferred sometimes on sinners, though the just are oftener made the partakers of it. The example of Balaam in the Old Testament, and that of Caiaphas in the New, show that God often selects persons of bad dispositions to declare his will. The examples of this may be few. The Church must be governed by certain rules respecting the gift of prophecy as well as the other extraordinary graces. It is not, when taken by itself, a mark of sanctity. The previous approbation of heroic virtues is more necessary when reference is made to visions and apparitions. Prophecies, miracles, and ecstasies can be proved by the testimony of those who have witnessed them. The certainty of visions and apparitions rests upon the deposition of those who have experienced them. They are witnesses in their own cause. They should be beyond every exception; their sanctity ought to be recognized. The heroism of their virtues must receive a favorable sentence. The virtues of the person and the effects which flow from it must be considered in judging of a supernatural apparition. Heroic virtues are what clearly show the nature of these. The exercise of the Christian virtues to an heroic degree are proved to satisfaction; after this an examination is made of the graces which are given gratuitously. They proceed to consider if they offer the true character of divine works. They are taken into account in the causes of canonization, as they are oftener conferred on saints than on sinners. The judges inquire if they have all the qualities requisite to attribute them to God. If these be found, and there is a probability that they come from him, they add a new lustre to them. The virtues which accompany them cause it to be seen that they have been conferred on the servant of God, not so much for the utility of others as to serve as witnesses for the sanctity of the servant of God. The theology of Salamanca says: "It cannot be denied but that virtues are a good previous disposition, and assist materially in the reception of them. It is on this account that they are more frequently granted to the just than to sinners. They hold the second rank after virtues in the canonization of saints. After this they proceed to an examination of the prophecies attributed to the servant of God. The heroism of the virtues must be proved to a certainty before they proceed to examine the revelations."

Three things must be considered in the examination of the prophecies. First, it must be seen—if what has been predicted is in conformity with the teaching of our Lord, of the apostles, and to the laws and discipline of the Church: if they be not conformable, although they may be justified by the event, they would do injury to the cause, instead of advancing it. It should be taken into account, in the second place, whether the circumstances which are included in the prophecy surpass human knowledge. It must also be shown that the event announced by the prophet, has been accomplished in the manner that has been predicted. This is not an essential mark of the truth of a prophecy, especially if it be of a threatening nature, or if it be doubtful. If the prophet has obeyed his own private instinct, instead of being the organ of the Holy Ghost—if he has not understood or announced things in accordance with the intentions of God—the event does not correspond with his words. The fact of this false prediction would not form an obstacle in the cause, though he would no longer be considered a true prophet. Ecstasies may come from a natural cause; it is therefore necessary to remark the supernatural signs, of which the cause may make mention. When these present really true signs—when they are united with heroic virtues fully accredited, they become like the other graces which are gratuitously given, indirect proofs of sanctity; this also applies to visions and apparitions. Revelations, prophecies, and other extraordinary graces of the servants of God, have a threefold relation with causes of canonization, and merit the consideration of the sacred congregation in a threefold point of view. The first is to see that there is nothing in them contrary to faith or morals, or that there is not contained in them a new doctrine, or what is not conformable to the common sentiment and practice of the Church. The second is, to inquire if the visions, the revelations, and the prophecies are supernatural, and deserve to be ranked among the gratuitous graces. The third is, to show that they may be tolerated, and also practised and approved of. The nature of this approbation has been already explained, and it is an event of a very rare occurrence.

We have already seen that saints may be in good faith and err in their revelations. They may suppose that their own conceptions are the inspiration of God. The example of St. Bernard shows that the saints may perform miracles, though they may be mistaken in their predictions respecting future events; this may arise from the following causes: They may not understand the subject they speak about, in accordance with the will of God; they may follow the inspirations of their own mind, and receive no illuminations from above. Their ecstasies may be only natural, and have nothing of the supernatural connected with them. God sometimes allows them to be exposed to ecstasies which have Satan for their author, in order to render them more humble. Demoniacal apparitions are frequently mentioned in the Lives of the Saints. Such being the state of the case, we may easily perceive with what circumspection we should receive the revelations and prophecies of those whose sanctity the Church has not recognized.

Theologians distinguish revelations into three classes—natural, demoniacal, and divine. The first arise from natural causes, bodily weakness, excessive watchings, a disturbed mind, or an ardent imagination; these act on the mind and make the person believe that they have revelations. The demoniacal come from the devil, who sometimes reveals certain things which are good. By this means he keeps a man from greater good, or leads him to destruction.

Contradictory and lying revelations come from the same source. Those which are useless or merely curious, without presenting matter for edification or instruction, have also Satan for their author. The too frequent repetition of revelations cause them to be suspected. What has been already stated will furnish sufficient means for us to discover false revelations and false prophecies. The marks of natural ecstasies are the same as those of the disease which causes them. If the person who has had the ecstasy is affected after it with paralysis, apoplexy, or any other disease, it is, no doubt, natural. If there be a weariness in the mind or in the body, a forgetfulness of what has passed, a sadness in the natural feelings, it may be ascribed to the same source. If violent desires for some worldly object, or the hearing of some sad and unexpected news precede the ecstasy, it may be attributed to a like cause. The marks of demoniacal ecstasies are varied. If the man follows a wicked life—if he falls into an ecstasy in an act of sin—it is, no doubt, the work of the devil. A contortion of the limbs, convulsions, an irregular movement of the body, are likewise signs of these ecstasies. Those which come when the person wills, and cease at his desire, must be from Satan. God never gives the heavenly gift after the manner of a habit, and grace draws the soul where it wills and as it wills. The person in an ecstasy who speaks with difficulty—as if he were compelled to speak, or as if another person spoke through him, or who forgets what he had said during the ecstasy, or who has them constantly and in public places before a great number of persons, is but the sport of the devil, who desires to seek his glory in external and striking things. *Martin del Rio* speaks of a girl who had ecstasies whenever she pleased; the Bishop of Saragossa discovered that these were the effect of a compact which she had entered into with the devil. Zachias relates that he saw a female who feigned ecstasies with such skill that the people believed they were real. They saw the arms extended, the eyes fixed during several hours, the lifting up of the body as if she would fly to heaven, the countenance in a moment changed into different colors. At one time she appeared as if she were dead; at the next she assumed her natural color. It is evidently from Satan if it suggests evil, or when the person is troubled in mind after it. In the time of St. Ignatius Loyola, there lived in Bologna a young person who endured such violent ecstasies that she became insensible to the heat of fire. She had the stigmata on her hands and her heart. Her head seemed pierced with thorns, and a great quantity of blood flowed from it. They inquired from the saint what he thought respecting it. He replied it might come from God, and it might come from the devil.

Apparitions and visions may be also either natural, demoniacal, or divine. Many natural causes may produce apparitions. The sick, the mad, persons disposed to melancholy, persons agitated with violent passions, can believe that they see many things which they have never seen, and will relate them as if they were visions which they had from heaven. Females are chiefly subject to these illusions; their temperament, their sensibility, and the ardor of their affections, make them consider as supernatural what exists only in their own mind. Every vision which a woman says she has, does not come from natural causes; they require, in consequence of the reasons already stated, a more careful examination.

We read in the visions of St. Augustine that St. Monica was much engaged with thinking on the marriage of her son, and that she desired to have a celestial vision respecting it. "She saw certain vain and fantastic things, and she related them to me, not with her usual confidence, but as if despising them." The saint was gifted with the spirit of discernment, and she knew the difference there is between those revelations which are the gift of God, and those which proceed from the thoughts of the mind; love of solitude often produces that state of mind from which natural visions proceed. When a person is in the habit of relating in an indiscreet manner revelations which he says he has, they should be looked upon with suspicion. Nothing is more opposed to the spirit of the saints, than to make known their revelations, their visions, and matters of this description. If they have been favored with these, they do all in their power to conceal them, and enjoin silence on those who become acquainted with them.

Demoniacal visions are far more dangerous than natural illusions. A fearful instance of these may be found in the 84th Homily of St. Antiochus: "There lived on Mount Sinai a monk, who gave a strong proof of his virtue by passing a great number of years in seclusion in a small cell. He was at last deceived by several false revelations from the devil, and by dreams. He fell into Judaism. The devil at first showed him several true apparitions in his dreams; by this means he gained power over his mind. He then showed him a great number of martyrs and Christians of every description; these spent their time in darkness without any light. The devil also showed him Moses, the prophets, and the Jewish people; these lived in a brilliant atmosphere, and were filled with every mark of joy and gladness. The unfortunate man fell away; he left the holy mountain and came to Palestine. He directed his steps to Noasa and Lybiadis, the asylum of the Jews; he told them of his demoniacal apparitions; he was circumcised, and professed Judaism. He preached publicly against the Christians, and endeavored to show that Judaism was now the favored religion of God. I knew him and most of the monks. Four years only have elapsed since his death." Such are the artifices of the devil. They have drawn into error even men of apparent virtue. Satan may suggest sometimes good things in his false apparitions. This is in order to prevent greater good. He will encourage persons to do some act of virtue, in order to deceive them more easily, and to lead them by degrees into a more fearful fall. The great preservative against so great dangers is prayer. The counsel of prudent men, and of those who are versed in the discernment of spirits, is also very advantageous.

The sanctity of those is very suspicious who give credence to their own revelations and apparitions, without consulting theologians or their confessors. There is much cause to fear that they are the victims of dangerous delusions. Christian prudence obliges them to submit every thing connected with these extraordinary manifestations to the judgment of those who can discern their true character. If these persons esteem it as probable that the revelations come from God, they cannot add it to the faith. The marks, the conjectures, and the arguments which establish the probability of a revelation, are not sufficient to make it an article of faith. "Probability," writes Benedict XIV., "is not sufficient. Evidence of a divine revelation is needed, that any person should be required to make an act of faith in it. This is more especially necessary if any thing is contained in it which is contrary to the precepts of God or the Church. If there is evidence of the revelation, and if a person knows for certain that it comes from God, the person who has received it is bound to add it to the faith. Those whom the revelation concerns, and to whom it is proposed or made known, are not obliged to believe it when it seems but probable. If it is certain and evident, they should obey and believe it; for when God speaks to them by another person, he requires that they believe on his word. Those to whom the revelation is not addressed are not obliged to believe it; if they do, they cannot give it divine faith. This requires the testimony of God himself, otherwise they would have the testimony of man for what God does not require them to believe. We suppose in this case that the revelation is not only probable, but is also certain and evident. We also take for granted that it has all the necessary marks of authenticity which can distinguish it from demoniacal and merely natural illusions. It should not be forgotten that wicked persons make use of the most shameful artifices to make others believe that they have had revelations and supernatural gifts, in order to obtain some unlawful end. Gravina cites many examples of this; Martin del Rio and other writers follow him in this respect. The following instance is taken from the *Spicilegium* of O. D'Achery; it goes as far back as the thirteenth century, and is called the Sibyl of Metz. The young person who passed by this name lived at Marsal, in the diocese of Metz. She saw many of the *Beguine* form themselves into a religious society, and she resolved to imitate them. She attended the churches regularly, even at the hour of matins, which were then celebrated at midnight, and also at the Mass. She conducted herself with such prudence that the curate of the parish, who was a wise man, and the entire population of the city, paid her the greatest veneration. She was received into a family who gave credence to her artifices, and enjoyed their hospitality. She made them believe that she had a vision of angels. She had appropriated to her use a room, in which she offered up her prayers and made her devotions. She saw herself becoming renowned in consequence of her piety, and she resolved to attempt something more remarkable. She gave out that she was caught up to heaven in a trance; she passed her days in bed, without eating or drinking. Her hostess, believing this, closed the door of her room, and allowed no person to enter it. The Sibyl, during the night, was accustomed to utter a slight groan; her hostess supposed that her spirit came back to her body at this time, and usually offered her something to eat; this she declined, saying she had received heavenly meat, and had given up worldly food. Some time after this it was discovered that a young man came to see her every night, and brought her food; he also gave her perfumes, which she spread through the room; she stated that the odor was caused by the visits of the angels. What she could not eat was carefully concealed in the bed, so that she had always enough of provisions for three or four days. She told the hostess not to be alarmed if she heard the doors opening during the night, as she was much tormented by the devil during the hours of darkness.

She had deceived everybody by her mode of acting. The Dominicans and Franciscans came to see her; they could not discover any deception; they praised her sanctity in their discourses. The Bishop of Metz paid her a visit. The nobility, the soldiers, the clergy, the monks, in short, all the inhabitants of the town, came in crowds. All, however, were not allowed to see her; for when she heard that so many persons called to see her, she pretended to be carried up to heaven in spirit, and could be seen by no person before three days. Those who had come from a distance, as soon as they léarned this, returned home and told these wonders to their friends and acquaintances. The Bishop of Metz and his clergy were anxious to know whether she really ate or drank; they had her removed to another house, where she would be placed more immediately under their own observation. She allowed no one to remain in her room during the night. She said the angels protected her against the assaults of the devil. She was under a great difficulty; for, as they watched her so closely, she could neither eat nor drink. In order to make them believe what she stated about the persecution of the devil, she pretended that she was in a trance; and getting up during the night, she took all the feathers out of her bed and scattered them about the house, while her guard slept. She believed that the devil did this in order to torment her; she had frequently said that she was tormented by him, and she stated that he had often done the same things. She had passed three days in this house without eating any thing, when she requested the Bishop to send her back to her former place, as she discovered, by a vision, that if she remained where she was, the devil would come and cut her body into small pieces. The Bishop acceded to her request. When the Sibyl perceived that the Bishop and the friars, by their giving credence to all that she said and did, added much to her fame, she resolved to attempt something more wonderful than any thing she had hitherto done. She made a black dress, with a hood; to this she added the face of a demon; she put this on whenever she pretended that she was in a trance; she spoke with a hoarse voice, and caused great terror in all those who came to see her; she sometimes, at night, left her room clad in her demoniacal costume, and went to several persons and spoke to them; they said it was the devil, who came to disturb the Sibyl; they all took flight, and she quietly returned to her chamber. One of the inhabitants, whose reputation was not of the best description, chanced to die; the Sibyl, when she heard of it, dressed herself in her costume and went to the house, and spoke in a hoarse voice to those who were there; she told them, in the name of the devil, that the Sibyl had taken away his friend, who had died that day. "She is in a trance for the last three days, and her prayers and meditations have effected this. I had fancied he belonged to me, and I wished to bring him to my prairie." They inquired where this was. She replied: "I have an extensive and beautiful prairie, where I bring my friends to enjoy themselves; it is covered with a sulphurous bath; in that place are vipers, serpents, buffaloes, and other large animals. I take pleasure with them, and my friends (my angels) plunge them into this bath. I could willingly tear in pieces this Sibyl, who has to-day deprived me of my friend, but I am afraid of the angels who are around her. When I return to my master, he will condemn me to the most frightful torments. I dare not, through this fear of her, abstain from telling you to take care of yourselves. You who listen to her will not come into this delightful prairie." The Bishop, and all who heard of this, believed that it was the devil who really made this address; they went to see the Sibyl, and found her lying in her bed; her face was

flushed, and she seemed to be asleep; her head was
covered with a cloth of so fine a texture that they
said no human hand could make any thing so fine;
her breathing was so gentle as to be scarcely per-
ceptible. Her hostess, in reply, stated that when
she came back from heaven, she was always clad in
finest linen. The Sibyl had told her that the angels
made her bed and gave her these presents; she had
also stated that the angels had blessed this water,
to enable her to overcome the attempts of the devil.
The hostess desired the Bishop and the friars to
drink the water and sprinkle themselves with it, to
preserve themselves from the devil. The Bishop
was thinking of building a church for her, where
the pilgrims might come and visit her. But her
deceptions were accidentally discovered; she had
declared that on a certain day she would have a
trance, and once more be taken up to heaven. The
doors of the house were closed; the persons who
lived there were asleep; she rises from her bed and
speaks in a hoarse tone, to personate the devil; she
suddenly changes her voice to imitate that of an
angel. Some who listened believed it to be a con-
troversy between Satan and an angel. One of the
friars, anxious to hear the nature of this, drew close
to the wall of the Sibyl's chamber, where he saw,
through a chink in the wall, the Sibyl, whom they
thought was in a trance, busily occupied in arrang-
ing her bed. Those who were there immediately
forced the door open, when she threw herself on
her bed. They roused her from her pretended

trance, and made her confess her artifices; they found provisions concealed in her bed; they saw the dress which she wore when she personated the devil, the hangings of her bed, and the various means she made use of to deceive the people. Those who were esteemed the wisest among the people were shocked at being made such dupes. Some were anxious that she should be burned, others that she should be put to death in a different way. The ecclesiastical authorities interfered, and she was consigned to prison, where she spent the remainder of her days.

Revelations of St. Bridget.

CHAPTER I.

PRAYER OF PRAISE AND THANKSGIVING, ON THE LIFE AND PASSION OF OUR LORD.

BLESSED art thou, my Lord, my God, and most beloved lover of my soul, who art one God in three persons. Glory and praise be to thee, O my Lord Jesus Christ, who wast sent by thy Father into the body of a Virgin, yet ever remainest with thy Father in heaven, the Father with his divinity remaining inseparably with thee in thy humanity in the world.

Honor and glory be to thee, O my Lord Jesus Christ, who, conceived of the Holy Ghost in the Virgin's womb, didst corporally increase, and humbly dwell therein, to the time of thy birth, and, after thy joyful nativity, didst deign to be handled by thy mother's most pure hands, be wrapped in swaddling-clothes, and laid in a manger.

Blessed art thou, my Lord Jesus Christ, who didst wish thy immaculate flesh to be circumcised, and thy name called Jesus, and also to be offered in the temple by thy Mother.

Blessed art thou, my Lord Jesus Christ, who caused thyself to be baptized in the Jordan, by thy servant John.

Blessed be thou, my Lord Jesus Christ, who didst preach with thy blessed lips the words of life to men; and didst work many miracles personally before them.

Blessed be thou, my Lord Jesus Christ, who, fulfilling the Scriptures of the prophets, didst reasonably show thyself to the world to be true God.

Benediction and glory be to thee, my Lord Jesus Christ, who didst wonderfully fast for forty days in the desert, and didst permit thyself to be tempted by thy enemy the devil, whom thou didst drive off by a single word, when so it pleased thee.

Blessed be thou, my Lord Jesus Christ, who didst foretell thy death before the time, and in the last supper didst wonderfully consecrate thy precious body of material bread, and also charitably gave it to thy Apostles, in memory of thy most worthy passion, and by washing their feet with thy sacred and precious hands, didst humbly show thy very great humility.

Honor be to thee, my Lord Jesus Christ, who through the fear of thy passion and death, didst send forth blood from thy body, and nevertheless didst perfect our redemption as thou didst wish to do, and thus didst more manifestly show the charity which thou didst bear the human race.

Glory be to thee, my Lord Jesus Christ, who, sold by thy disciple, and bought by the Jews, was seized for us, and who didst cast thy enemies to the ground by a single word, and didst afterwards, of thy free will, give thyself up a captive to their unclean, rapacious hands.

Blessed be thou, my Lord Jesus Christ, who wast led to Caiphas, and who, though judge of all, didst humbly permit thyself to be given up to the judgment of Pilate.

Blessed be thou, my Lord Jesus Christ, who wast sent by Pilate the judge, to Herod, and didst suffer thyself to be derided and despised by him, and didst consent to be sent back again to Pilate as judge.

Glory be to thee, my Lord Jesus Christ, for

the derision which thou didst undergo, when, clothed in purple, thou didst stand, crowned with most acute thorns; and, because thou didst most patiently bear to be spit upon, in thy glorious face, thy eyes bound, and to be most violently beaten on the cheeks and neck, by the malignant hands of the wicked.

Peace be to thee, my Lord Jesus Christ, who didst most patiently suffer thyself to be bound to a pillar, inhumanly scourged, led, streaming with blood, to Pilate's tribunal, and to be seen like an innocent lamb.

Blessed be thou, my Lord Jesus Christ, who didst most patiently submit to hear, with thy blessed ears, insults and lies vomited against thee, and the voices of the people asking that a guilty robber should be absolved, and thou, innocent, condemned.

Honor be to thee, my Lord Jesus Christ, who, with thy whole glorious body bathed in blood, was condemned to die on the cross, and didst painfully bear thy cross on thy sacred shoulders, and wast furiously led to the place of thy passion, and despoiled of thy garments, and didst thus wish to be fastened to the cross.

Immense glory be to thee, my Lord Jesus Christ, who didst humbly bear for us, that the

Jews should extend thy venerable hands and feet with a robe, and cruelly fasten thee to the wood of the cross with iron nails, and should call thee a betrayer; and writing a title of confusion above thee, should in manifold ways deride thee with their horrid words.

Eternal praise and thanksgiving be to thee, my Lord Jesus Christ, who didst so meekly endure such cruel pains for us; for when thy blessed body lost all its strength on the cross, thy blessed eyes were darkened, thy beautiful face, from loss of blood, was all overspread with pallor, thy blessed tongue was parched and dried up, and thy mouth was moistened by a most bitter draught. Thy hair and beard were filled with blood, from the wounds of thy most sacred head. The bones of thy hands and feet, and of all thy precious body, were rent from their places, not without great and intense grief to thee, the veins and nerves of all thy blessed body were cruelly broken. And thus thou wast inhumanly scourged and wounded with grievous wounds, that thy most innocent skin and flesh were intolerably torn. And thus afflicted and tortured, thou didst hang on the cross, O my most sweet Jesus, and in excessive pain. didst patiently and humbly await the hour of death.

Perpetual honor be to thee, my Lord Jesus Christ, who, in such agony, didst humbly look with benign eyes of charity on thy most worthy Mother, who never sinned, nor consented to even the slightest sin, and consoling her, didst faithfully commit her to the guardianship of thy disciple.

Eternal benediction be to thee, my Lord Jesus Christ, for each hour in which thou didst endure the most intense bitterness and agony on the cross, for us sinners. For the acute pain of thy wounds keenly penetrated thy happy soul, and cruelly pierced thy most sacred heart, till thy heart breaking, thou didst happily give up the ghost, and bowing down thy head, didst humbly commend thyself into the hands of God, thy Father, and then thy dead body remained all cold.

Blessed be thou, my Lord Jesus Christ, who, for our salvation, didst permit thy side and heart to be pierced with a lance, and didst send forth copiously from the same side thy precious blood and water to redeem us; and didst not wish thy most sacred body to be taken down from the cross, till permission was given by the judge.

Glory be to thee, my Lord Jesus Christ, because thou didst wish thy blessed body to be taken down from the cross by thy friends, and to be laid in the arms of thy most afflicted mother, and didst permit it to be wrapped by her in winding-sheets, and laid in the sepulchre, and there to be guarded by soldiers.

Eternal honor be to thee, my Lord Jesus Christ, who didst rise from the dead on the third day, and didst manifest thyself alive to such as thou didst wish; and after forty days, didst ascend in the sight of many to heaven, and didst there honorably place thy friends whom thou hadst delivered from limbo.

Eternal praise and jubilee be to thee, my Lord Jesus Christ, who didst send down thy Holy Spirit into the hearts of thy disciples, and didst augment in their spirits immense divine love.

Blessed be thou, and pleased and glorious forever, my Lord Jesus, who sittest on the throne in thy kingdom of heaven, in the glory of thy divinity, living corporally with all thy most holy members, which thou didst assume of the flesh of a Virgin. And thus thou wilt come on the day of judgment to judge the souls of all, living and dead. Who livest and reignest with the Father and Holy Ghost, for ever and ever. Amen.

CHAPTER II.

PRAYER OF PRAISE AND THANKSGIVING, ON THE LIFE OF THE BLESSED VIRGIN.

BLESSED and venerated be thou, my Lady Virgin Mary, most holy Mother of God, whose noblest creature thou art, and who was never so closely loved as by thee, O glorious Lady.

Glory be to thee, my Lady Virgin Mary, Mother of God, who by the same angel, by whom Christ was announced to thee, was announced to thy father and mother, and wast conceived and born in their most holy union.

Blessed be thou, my Lady Virgin Mary, who in thy most holy infancy, immediately after being weaned, wast borne by thy parents to God's temple, and committed, with other virgins, to the care of the devout high priest.

Praise be to thee, my Lady Virgin Mary, who when thou didst attain an age to know that God, thy Creator, existed, didst immediately begin to love him intensely, above all things, and didst then most discreetly order thy day and night, in different offices and exercises to the honor of God; and didst so curtail the food and sleep of thy glorious body as to be apt to serve God.

Infinite glory be to thee, my Lady Virgin Mary, who didst humbly vow thy virginity to God, and, therefore, didst not care who espoused thee, because thou didst know, that he to whom thou didst first pledge thy faith, was more powerful and better than all.

Blessed be thou, my Lady Virgin Mary, who wast alone inflamed with the ardor of divine love, contemplating with all thy mind, and with all the elevated virtue of thy powers, the most high God, to whom with ardent love thou hadst offered thy virginity, when the angel of God was sent to thee, and saluting thee, announced to thee the will of God. To whom, thou replying, didst most humbly declare thyself the handmaid of God; and the Holy Ghost wonderfully filled thee with all virtue. God the Father sent thee his coeternal and coequal Son, who, coming in thee, then assumed to himself a human body of thy flesh and blood. And so, in that blessed hour, the Son of God became in thee thy son, living with all his members, yet not losing his divine Majesty.

Blessed be thou, my Lady Virgin Mary, who didst constantly feel the body of Christ, created of thy blessed body, grow and move in thy womb till the time of his glorious nativity. Whom thou before all others didst touch with thy sacred hands, wrap up in clothes, and, according to the oracle of the prophet, didst lay in a manger, and didst maternally nurture him with the sacred milk of thy blessed breasts, in great joy of exultation.

Glory be to thee, O my Lady Virgin Mary, who, inhabiting a contemptible house,—a stable,—didst see powerful kings come from afar, to thy Son, humbly offering royal gifts with great reverence to thy Son. Whom afterwards thou didst present with thy precious hands in the Temple, and didst diligently lay up in thy blessed heart all things seen and heard in his infancy.

Blessed be thou, my Lady Virgin Mary, who didst fly to Egypt with thy most holy Son, whom thou didst afterwards bring with joy to Nazareth, and behold him, thy Son, as he increased bodily, humble and obedient to thee and Joseph.

Blessed be thou, my Lady Virgin Mary, who didst behold thy Son preaching, working miracles, and choosing his Apostles, who, enlightened by his example, miracles, and doctrine, were made witnesses of the truth, announcing to all nations that thy Jesus was truly the Son of God, that it was he who had accomplished in himself the oracles of the prophets, when he had patiently endured a most atrocious death for the human race.

Blessed be thou, my Lady Virgin Mary, who didst long beforehand know that thy Son was to be arrested, and didst afterwards, with thy blessed eyes, mournfully see him bound and scourged, crowned with thorns, and fastened naked to the cross, and many despising him and calling him a seducer.

Honor be to thee, my Lady Virgin Mary, who didst painfully hear with thy blessed ears thy Son speaking to thee in pain from the cross,. and crying to the Father in the agony of death, and commending his soul to his Father's hands.

Praise be to thee, my Lady Virgin Mary, who in bitter grief didst behold thy Son hanging on the cross, livid and stained with his own blood from the top of his head to the sole of his feet, and thus cruelly die. And didst most bitterly see his feet and hands, together with his glorious side, transpierced, and his whole skin torn without any mercy.

Blessed be thou, my Lady Virgin Mary,

who with tearful eyes didst behold thy Son taken down, wrapped in winding-sheets, laid in the sepulchre, and there guarded by soldiers.

Blessed be thou, my Lady Virgin Mary, who didst depart from the sepulchre of thy Son, with intense grief of thy deeply wounded heart, and wast borne, all full of grief, to John's house by thy friends, and didst there immediately feel a relief of thy great grief, because thou didst most certainly foreknow that he would quickly rise again.

Rejoice, my most worthy Lady Virgin Mary, that the very moment thy Son rose from the dead, he wished this to be known to thee, his most blessed Mother, because he at once appeared in person to thee, then showed to others that he was risen from the dead, who underwent death in his living body.

Rejoice, then, my most worthy Lady Virgin Mary, who, death being conquered, and the agent of death supplanted and the way of heaven laid open, didst see thy Son rising triumphant with the crown of victory; and on the fortieth day after his resurrection, didst behold him honorably ascend in the sight o many, to his heavenly kingdom, attended like a king by angels.

Exult, my most worthy Lady Virgin Mary, that thou didst deserve to see how thy Son, after his ascension, sent down on his Apostles and disciples the Holy Ghost, wherewith he had already filled thee entirely; and increasing in them the fervor of charity and uprightness of Catholic faith, wonderfully enlightened their hearts.

Rejoice, especially, my Lady Virgin Mary, and let the whole earth rejoice with thy joy, that thy Son permitted thee to remain many years in this world after his ascension, to console his friends and strengthen them in faith, to help the needy, and sagely counsel the Apostles.

And then, by thy most prudent words, most virtuous behavior, and holy deeds, he converted to the Catholic faith innumerable Jews and Pagan infidels, and wonderfully enlightened them to confess thee to be his Virgin Mother, and himself thy Son, and God with a real humanity.

Blessed be thou, my Lady Virgin Mary, who from thy ardent charity and maternal love didst unceasingly, hour by hour, desire to go to thy beloved Son, now sitting in heaven; and thou living in this world, by sighing for heavenly things, didst humbly conform thyself to the divine will, whereby, as divine justice dictated, thou didst unspeakably increase thy eternal glory.

Eternal honor and glory be to thee, my Lady Virgin Mary, who, when it pleased God to take thee from the exile of this world, and to honor thy soul eternally in his kingdom, vouchsafed to announce it to thee by his angel, and who wished thy venerable body, when dead, to be interred by the Apostles, with all reverence, in the sepulchre.

Rejoice, O my Lady Virgin Mary, that in thy calm death thy soul was embraced by the power of God, who paternally guarding it, protected it from all adversity. And then God the Father subjected all that is created to thy power; and the Son of God most honorably placed thee, his most worthy mother, on a most exalted throne beside him; and the Holy Ghost wonderfully exalted thee to his glorious kingdom, a Virgin espoused to himself.

Rejoice eternally, my Lady Virgin Mary, that for some days after thy death, thy body lay buried in the tomb, until, by the power of God, it was again honorably united to thy soul.

Exult, O mother of God, glorious Lady

Virgin Mary, that thou didst deserve to see thy soul quickened after death, assumed with thy soul with angelic honors to heaven, and didst see thy glorious Son, God with humanity, and with exulting joy behold him to be the most just judge of all men, and the rewarder of good works.

Rejoice also, my Lady Virgin Mary, that the sacred flesh of thy body knew that it existed Virgin Mother in heaven, and saw itself immaculate from all mortal and venial stain; nay, knew that thou hadst done all virtuous deeds so in love that it behooved God to honor thee with the highest honor. Then also didst thou understand, that whoso loves God more ardently in this world, will be placed nearer to himself by God, in heaven. And as it was manifest to all the court of heaven that no one, of angels or of men, loved God with as much charity as thou, therefore it was just and worthy that God himself should honorably place thee, soul and body, on the highest seat of glory.

Blessed be thou, O my Lady Virgin Mary, that every faithful creature praises the Trinity for thee, because thou art his most worthy creature; who, dost most promptly obtain pardon for wretched souls, and art the most faithful advocate and pleader for all sinners.

Praised then be God, supreme Emperor and Lord, who created thee to so great honor, that thou shouldst become perennially Empress and Lady in the kingdom of heaven, to reign with him eternally through ages of ages. Amen.

CHAPTER III.

THE IMMACULATE CONCEPTION.

The Blessed Virgin speaks.

AND it is a truth that I was conceived without original sin, and not in sin; because, as my Son and I never sinned, so no marriage was more holy than that from which I was born. —Lib. vi., c. 49.

A golden hour was my conception, for then began the principle of the salvation of all, and darkness hastened to light. God wished to do in his work something singular and hidden from the world, as he did in the dry rod blooming. But know that my conception was not known to all, because God wished that as the natural law and the voluntary election of good and bad preceded the written law, and the written law followed, restraining all inordinate notions, so it pleased God, that his friends should piously doubt of my conception, and that each should show his zeal till the truth became clear in its preordained time.— Lib. vi., c. 55.

CHAPTER IV.

BIRTH OF THE BLESSED VIRGIN.

When I was born, it was not unknown to the demons, but speaking by a certain similitude, they thus thought: "So a certain virgin is born, what shall we do? For it is evident that something wonderful is to take place in her. If we throw around her all the nets of our malice, she will burst them like tow. If we examine all her heart, it is defended by a strong garrison. There is no spot in her for a spear to touch. Therefore, we may fear lest her purity be our torture. Her grace will crush all our strength; her constancy prostrate us beneath her feet." But the friends of God, who were in long expectation, said by divine inspiration: "Why grieve we more? We should rather rejoice, for the light is born that is to dispel our darkness, and our desire shall be accomplished." And the angels of God rejoiced, although their joy was always in the vision of God, saying: "Something desirable is born on earth, and especially beloved by God, whereby true peace shall be restored to heaven and earth, and our losses shall be made up." Indeed, daughter, I assure thee, that my birth was the opening of true joy; for then came forth the rod from which that flower proceeded, whom kings and prophets desired. And when I had attained an age to know something of my Creator, then I turned to him with unspeakable love, and desired him with my whole heart. I was also preserved by wonderful grace, so that not even in my tender years did I consent to sin, because the love of God and my parents' care, good education, the preservation of good, and fervor of knowing God preserved with me.—Lib. vi., c. 56.

I am she, who from eternity have been in the love of God, and from my infancy the Holy Ghost was perfectly with me. And you may take an example from a nut, which, when it grows exteriorly, increases in the interior, so that the shell is always full, and there is no space to receive aught else. So I, from my childhood, was full of the Holy Ghost, and according to the increase of my body and age, the Holy Ghost filled me so copiously as to leave no room for the entrance of any sin. Hence I never committed a mortal or venial sin, for I was so ardent in the love of God, that nothing was pleasing to me except the perfect will of God; for the fire of divine love was enkindled in my soul, and God, blessed above all who created me by his power, and filled me with the virtue of the Holy Ghost, had an ardent love for me.—Lib. iii., c. 8.

CHAPTER V.

EARLY LIFE OF THE BLESSED VIRGIN.

As soon as I understood that there was a God, I was always solicitous and fearful for my salvation and observance. And when I heard more fully that God was, too, my Creator, and judge of all my actions, I loved him intensely, and every hour feared and pondered lest I should offend him in word or deed. Then when I heard that he had given a law to his people, and his commandments, and wrought so many wonders with them, I firmly resolved in my mind to love naught but him, and all worldly things became most bitter to me. Hearing after this that this same God was to redeem the world and be born of a virgin, I was filled with such love for her, that I thought of naught but God, wished naught but him. I withdrew as much as possible from the converse and presence of kindred and friends. All that I could have I gave to the poor, reserving to myself only scanty food and clothing. Nothing pleased me but God. Ever did I long in my heart to live to the time of his birth, if perchance I might be worthy to be the unworthy handmaid of the mother of God. I also vowed in my heart to observe virginity if it was pleasing to him, and to possess nothing in the world. But if God willed otherwise, that his will, not mine, be done; because I believed him omnipotent, and desirous of naught but my good, so that I committed my will absolutely to him.

As the time approached, when by rule, virgins were presented in the Temple of the Lord, I went up among them in submission to my parents, thinking that nothing was impossible to God. And as he knew that I desired nothing, wished nothing but himself, he could, if it pleased him, preserve me in my virginity, if not, his will be done. After hearing all the instructions in the Temple, I returned home, inflamed with still greater love of God, enkindled daily by new fervor and desire of love. I accordingly retired apart from all more than usual, and I was alone night and day fearing most intensely lest tongue should speak or ear hear aught against my God, or eyes see aught delightful. Even in my silence was I timid and most anxious, lest I should be silent when I ought rather to speak. When I was thus troubled in heart alone by myself, and committed all my hope to God, at once it came into my mind to think of God's great power, how the angels and all things created serve him, and what his glory, which is ineffable and interminable. For I saw the sun, but not as it shines in heaven; I saw light, but not such light as shines in the world. I perceived an odor, not like that of plants or any thing of the kind, but most sweet and almost ineffable with which I was all filled, and exulted for joy. Then immediately I heard a voice, but from no human lips. And on hearing it I feared considerably, thinking with myself whether it was an illusion, and forthwith an angel of God appeared before me, like a most beautiful man, but not clothed in flesh, who said to me: Hail, Mary, &c. When I heard this, I wondered what this meant, or why he uttered such a salutation; for I knew myself, and deemed myself unworthy of this or of any good. But it is not impossible to God to do whatsoever he willeth. Then the angel said again: What is born in thee is holy, and shall be called the Son of God; and as it shall please him, so shall it be done. Still I deemed myself unworthy, and asked the angel not why or when, but how it should be done, that I, unworthy, should be the mother of God, not knowing man. And the angel answered me as I said: Nothing is impossible to God, but whatsoever he willeth shall come to pass, &c. Hearing the words of the angel, I felt a most fervent desire to be the mother of God, and my soul spoke in love: Here I am, let thy will be done in me. At this word my Son was instantly conceived in my womb, with unspeakable exultation of my soul and my whole body. And when I had him in my womb, I bore him without pain, without any weight or feeling of inconvenience. In all things I humbled myself, knowing that he was almighty whom I bore. And when I brought him forth, I brought him forth without pain and sin, as I conceived him, with such exultation of soul and body, that for exultation my feet did not feel the ground they stood upon. And as he entered all my members with the joy of my whole soul, so with the joy of my whole body, my soul exulting with ineffable joy, he came forth, my virginity untouched. And when I beheld him and considered his beauty, my soul in joy distilled, as it were, dew, knowing myself unworthy of such a Son. But when I considered the places of the nails in his hands and feet, which according to the prophets, I heard were to be crucified, then my eyes filled with tears and my heart was breaking with sadness. And when my Son gazed into my streaming eyes, he was sorrowful unto death. But when I considered the power of his deity, I was again consoled, knowing that he so willed it, and that so it was expedient, and I conformed my will to his will, and thus my joy was tempered by pain.

CHAPTER VI.

THE VISITATION.

When the angel announced to me that I should bear a Son, as soon as I consented, I felt something amazing and inexplicable in me, so that greatly wondering, I at once went up to my cousin Elizabeth to console her in her pregnancy and confer with her on what the angel had announced to me. And when she met me at the well, and we enjoyed each other's embrace and kiss, the infant in her womb, by a wonderful and visible motion, rejoiced. And I likewise was then moved in my heart by unwonted exultation, so that my tongue spoke unpremeditated words of God, and my soul could scarce contain itself for joy. And when Elizabeth wondered at the fervor of spirit that spoke in me, and I not otherwise wondered at the grace of God in her, we remained together many days blessing God. And after this a certain thought began to impress my mind, how and how devoutly I should act after so great a favor bestowed on me. What should I reply, if asked how I conceived, or who was the father of the Son I was to bear; or lest perchance Joseph, instigated by the enemy, should suspect me of evil. While thinking of these things, an angel, not unlike the one whom I had seen before, stood by me, saying: "Our God, who is eternal, is with thee and in thee. Fear not then, he will give thee to speak, he will direct thy steps and abode. He will perfect his work with thee powerfully and wisely." But Joseph, to whom I had been confided, when he perceived me to be pregnant, wondering and thinking himself unworthy to dwell with me, was troubled, not knowing what to do, till the angel told him in sleep: "Depart not from the virgin confided to thee, for it is most true as thou hast heard from her; for she has conceived of the Spirit of God, and shall bear a Son, the Saviour of the world. Therefore, serve her faithfully, and be thou the guardian and witness of her purity." Then from that day Joseph served me as his lady, and I humbled myself to his lowest labor. After this I was constantly in prayer, rarely wishing to see or be seen, and most rarely going forth, unless to the appointed feasts; and I was assiduous in the watches and readings given by our priests. I had a fixed time for manual labor, and I was discreet in fasting as much as my constitution could bear in God's service. Whatever we had over our daily sustenance we gave to the poor, content with what we had. Joseph so served me, that no scurrilous, murmuring, or angry word was heard from him, for he was most patient in poverty, solicitous in labor when it was necessary, most mild to those who reproached, most obedient in my service, a most prompt defender against those who gainsayed my virginity, a most faithful witness of the wonders of God. For he was so dead to the world and the flesh that he never desired aught but heavenly things. And so confident was he in God's promises, that he would constantly exclaim: Would that I could live to see God's will fulfilled. Most rarely did he go to gatherings of men and their councils, because his whole desire was to obey the will of God, and therefore is his glory now so great.—Lib. vi., c. 59.

CHAPTER VII.

HER LIFE WITH ST. JOSEPH.

The Blessed Virgin speaks.

KNOW most certainly that before he married me, Joseph knew in the Holy Ghost, that I had vowed my virginity to my God, and was immaculate in thought, word, and deed, and that he espoused me with the intention of serving me, holding me in the light of a sovereign mistress, not a wife. And I knew most certainly in the Holy Ghost that my perpetual virginity would remain intact, although by a secret dispensation of God I was married to a husband. But when I had consented to the ⁀ununciation of God, Joseph, seeing my womb increase by the operation of the Holy Ghost, feared vehemently; not suspecting any thing amiss in me, but remembering the sayings of the prophets, foretelling that the Son of God should be born of a virgin, deeming himself unworthy to serve such a 'mother, until the angel in a dream ordered him not to fear, but to minister unto me in charity.

Of worldly things Joseph and I reserved naught to ourselves, except the necessaries of life for the honor of God, distributing the rest for the love of God.

When the time of my Son's nativity approached, I came according to the foreknowledge of God to Bethlehem, bringing a most clean dress and clothes for my Son, which no one had ever used. In these I first wrapped him who was born of me in all purity, and although from all eternity I was ordained to sit on the highest throne and honor, yet in my humility, I did not disdain to prepare and minister what was necessary for Joseph and myself.—Lib. vii., c. 35.

CHAPTER VIII.

THE NATIVITY.

When I was at the crib of Bethlehem, I beheld a most beautiful Virgin with child, in a white mantle and tunic, evidently soon about to be delivered. With her was a most venerable old man, and they had an ox and an ass. When they entered the cave, the old man tied the ox and the ass to the crib, going out he brought the Virgin a lighted torch, and set it in the wall. Then he again withdrew so as not to be personally present at the birth. Then the Virgin loosed her shoes from off her feet, and laid aside her white mantle, and took off her veil from her head, and laid it beside her, remaining in her tunic, her long hair, as beautiful as gold, falling down over her shoulders. Then she drew out two fine, clean linen cloths, and two of wool, which she had brought to wrap the new-born child in, and two smaller linen ones to cover and tie his head. These she laid beside her to use in due time. When all these things were ready, then the Virgin, kneeling with great reverence, placed herself in prayer, with her back to the crib, her face eastward, raised to heaven. She stood with uplifted hands, and eyes fixed on heaven, rapt as it were, in an ecstasy of contemplation, inebriated with the divine sweetness. And while she thus stood in prayer, I beheld her child move in her womb, and at once in a moment, and in the twinkling of an eye, she brought forth her Son, from whom such ineffable light and splendor radiated, that the sun could not be compared to it; nor did the torch which the old man had set, in any manner give light, because that divine splendor had totally annihilated the material splendor of the torch, and so sudden and momentary was that mode of bearing, that I could not perceive or discern how, or in what part she brought forth. Nevertheless, I immediately beheld that glorious babe lying naked and most pure on the ground, his flesh most clean from all filth or impurity. . . . . I then also heard angelic chants of wonderful suavity and great sweetness. . . . . When the Virgin perceived that she had been delivered, she immediately bowed her head, and joining her hands, adored her Son with great respect and reverence, saying: "Welcome, my God, and my Lord, and my Son." Then the child crying, and, as it were, shivering with cold and the hard floor where he lay, turned a little, and stretched out his limbs, seeking to find a mother's favor and caress. Then his mother took him in her hands and clasped him to her heart, and with her cheek and breast warmed him with great joy, and a mother's tender compassion. Then sitting on the ground, she laid her son in her lap, ... and began diligently to wrap him up, at first in linen and then in woollen cloths, and drawing them tight on his little body, bound his legs and arms with fillets tied to the four corners of the outer woollen cloth. And then she wrapped on her Son's head the two small linen cloths, which she had ready for the purpose. When this was done, the old man entered, and prostrating himself on his knees on the ground, he adored him, weeping for joy. Nor did the Virgin on this occasion lose color or strength, as befalls other women who are delivered, except that her size was diminished. Then she arose with the child in her arms, and both together, that is, she and Joseph, laid him in the manger, and kneeling, adored him with immense joy and gladness.—Lib. vii., c. 21.

The Blessed Virgin speaks.

My daughter, know that I bore my Son as you have seen, praying alone on my knees in the stable. I bore him with such joy and exultation of mind, that I felt no pain or difficulty when he left my body. But I immediately wrapped him up in clean swaddling-clothes which I had previously prepared. When Joseph saw this, he wondered with great joy, that I had been delivered without any aid; but as the great multitude of people in Bethlehem was busy with the census, the wonders of God could not be divulged among them. And therefore, know truly, that although men, according to human ideas, would assert that my Son was born in the usual way, it is true beyond all doubt, that he was born as I tell thee and thou hast seen.—Lib. vii., c. 23.

While the Blessed Virgin and Joseph were adoring the infant in the crib, I beheld the shepherds, and those that tended the flocks, come to see and adore the child. When they saw him, they immediately adored him with great reverence and joy; and afterwards returned, praising and glorifying God for all that they had heard and seen.—Lib. vii., c. 23.

The Blessed Virgin speaks.

Daughter, know that when the three royal Magi came into the stable to adore my Son, I knew of their coming by prescience. And when they entered and adored him, then my Son exulted, and for joy wore a more cheerful countenance. I, too, rejoiced and exulted in wonderful joy of mind; observing their words and actions, retaining them and laying them up in my heart.—Lib. vii., c. 24.

CHAPTER IX.

THE PURIFICATION.

I DID not need purification, like other women, because my son who was born of me, made me clean. Nor did I contract the least stain, who bore my most pure Son without any stain. Nevertheless, that the law and the prophecies might be fulfilled, I chose to live according to the law. Nor did I live like worldly parents, but humbly conversed with the humble. Nor did I wish to show any thing extraordinary in me, but loved whatever was humble. On that day as to-day was my pain increased. For though, by divine inspiration, I knew that my Son was to suffer, yet this grief pierced my heart more keenly at Simeon's words, when he said that a sword should pierce my soul, and that my Son should be set for a sign to be contradicted. And until I was assumed in body and soul to heaven, this grief never left my heart, although it was tempered by the consolation of the spirit of God. I also wish you to know that from that day my grief was sixfold. The first was in my knowledge: for every time that I looked upon my Son, wrapped him in his swaddling-clothes, or gazed upon his hands and feet, so often was my soul swallowed up, as it were, by fresh grief, for I thought how he was to be crucified. In the second place, there was pain in my hearing: for as often as I heard the opprobriums heaped on my Son, the falsehoods uttered against him, the snares laid for him, my soul was so afflicted, that I could scarcely contain myself; but by the power of God, my grief knew bounds and respect, so that no impatience or levity was seen in me. In the third place, I suffered by sight: for when I beheld my Son bound and scourged, and suspended on the cross, I fell, as it were, lifeless; but recovering myself, I stood mourning and suffering so patiently, that neither my enemies nor any others beheld any thing but gravity in me. My fourth suffering was in the touch: for I with others took my Son down from the cross, wrapped him up, and laid him in the tomb; and thus my grief increased, so that my hands and feet had scarce strength to bear me. Oh, how gladly would I then have been laid beside my Son! Fifthly, I suffered by a vehement desire of joining my Son, after he ascended to heaven; because the long delay which I had in this world, after his Ascension, increased my grief. Sixthly, I suffered from the tribulations of the Apostles and friends of God, ever fearing and grieving: fearing that they might yield to temptations and tribulations; grieving because my Son's words were everywhere contradicted. But though the grace of God always persevered with me, and my will always conformed to the will of God, yet my grief was constantly mingled with consolation, till I was assumed, body and soul, to my Son in heaven. Let not, then, this grief leave thy heart, for without tribulation few would reach heaven.—Lib. vi., c. 57.

CHAPTER X.

ON THE FLIGHT INTO EGYPT.

Jesus saith: Why did I flee into Egypt? I answer: Before the fall, there was one way to heaven, broad and clear: broad in the abundance of virtues, clear in the divine wisdom and the obedience of a good will. Then the will being changed, there were two ways, one leading to heaven, the other from it; obedience led to heaven, disobedience seduced. As the choice of good and evil, obedience and disobedience, because he wished otherwise than God wished him to wish. To save man, it was right and just, that one should come who might redeem him, and be possessed of perfect obedience and charity; and in whom those who wish might show charity, and those who wished, malice. But no angel could be sent to redeem man, because I, God, gave not my glory to another, nor was a man found who could appease me for himself, still less for others. Hence I, sole just God, came to justify all.

By my flight to Egypt, I showed the infirmities of my humanity, and fulfilled the prophecies; I gave, too, an example to my disciples, that sometimes persecution is to be avoided for the greater future glory of God. That I was not found by my pursuers, the counsel of my Deity prevailed over man's counsel, for it is not easy to fight against God. That the innocents were slain, was a sign of my future passion, a mystery of those to be called, and of divine charity; for though the innocents did not bear testimony unto me by voice and mouth, yet they did by their death, as agreed with my childhood; because it was foreseen, that even in the blood of innocents, praise should be perfected to God. For though the malice of the unjust unjustly afflicted them, yet my divine permission, ever just and benignant, exposed them only justly, to show the malice of men and the incomprehensible counsel and piety of my divinity. Therefore, when unjust malice wreaked itself on the children, there justly superabounded merit and grace; and where the confession of the tongue and age were wanting, there the blood shed accumulated the most perfect good.— Lib. v., inter. xii., sol. 4.

CHAPTER XI.

THE LIFE OF JESUS BEFORE HIS PASSION.

MARY speaketh: I have spoken to thee of my dolors; but that dolor was not the least which I experienced, when I bore my Son in my flight to Egypt, and when I heard the innocents slaughtered, and Herod pursuing my Son. But, although I knew what was written of my Son, yet my heart, for the excessive love I bore my Son, was filled with grief and sadness. You may perhaps ask what my Son did all that time of his life before his Passion. I reply, that, as the Gospel says, he was subject to his parents, and he acted like other children, till he reached his majority. Nor were wonders wanting in his youth: how idols were silenced, and fell in numbers in Egypt at his coming; how the Wise Men foretold that my Son should be a sign of great things to come; how, too, the ministries of angels appeared; how, too, no uncleanness appeared upon him, nor entanglement in his hair, all which it is unnecessary for thee to know, as signs of his divinity and humanity are set forth in the Gospel, which may edify thee and others. But when he came to more advanced years, he was in constant prayer, and obediently went up with us to Jerusalem and elsewhere, to the appointed feasts; so wonderful then were his sight and words, and so acceptable, that many in affliction, said: "Let us go to Mary's Son, by whom we may be consoled." But increasing in age and wisdom, wherewith he was replete from the first, he labored with his hands, in such things as were becoming, and spoke to us separately words of consolation and divinity, so that we were continually filled with unspeakable joy. But when we were in fear, poverty, and difficulty, he did not make for us gold and silver, but exhorted us to patience, and we were wonderfully preserved from the envious. Necessaries were occasionally furnished to us by the compassion of pious souls, sometimes from our own labor, so that we had what was necessary for our actual support, but not for superfluity, for we only sought to serve God. After this, he conversed familiarly with friends who came to the house, on the law, and its meanings and figures; he also openly disputed with the learned, so that they wondered, saying: "Ho! Joseph's Son teaches the masters, some great spirit speaketh in him." Once as I was thinking of his Passion, seeing my sadness, he said: "Dost thou not believe, mother, that I am in the Father, and the Father in me? Wast thou sullied when I entered thee, or in pain when I came forth? Why art thou contracted by sadness? For it is the will of my Father, that I suffer death; nay, my will with the Father. What I have of the Father cannot suffer; but the flesh which I took of thee shall suffer, that the flesh of others may be redeemed, and their spirits saved." He was so obedient, that when Joseph by chance said: Do this or that, he immediately did it, because he so concealed the power of his divinity, that it could not be discerned except by me, and sometimes by Joseph, who both often saw an admirable light poured around him, and heard angelic voices singing over him. We also saw that unclean spirits, which could not be expelled by tried exorcists in our law, departed at the sight of my Son's presence.

CHAPTER XII.

OUR LORD'S APPEARANCE.

SUCH as my Son is in heaven you cannot behold. But hear what he was in body in the world. He was so beautiful of countenance, that no one looked him in the face without being consoled by his aspect, even if heartbroken with grief. The just were consoled with spiritual consolation; and even the bad were relieved from worldly sadness as long as they gazed upon him. Hence, those in grief were wont to say: "Let us go and see Mary's Son; we shall be relieved for that time."

In his twentieth year he was perfect in manly strength and stature. Amid those of modern times he would be large, not fleshy, but of large frame and muscle. His hair, eyebrows, and beard, were of a light brown; his beard a hand's width long. His forehead not prominent or retreating, but erect. His nose moderate, neither small nor large; his eyes were so pure, that even his enemies delighted to look upon him; his lips not thick, but clear red. His chin was not prominent or over long, but graceful in beautiful moderation. His cheeks modestly fleshy, his complexion clear white and red. His bearing erect, and his whole body spotless.—Lib. iv., c. 70.

CHAPTER XIII.

THE BAPTISM OF OUR LORD IN THE JORDAN.

Jesus speaketh: Why did I choose to be baptized? Whoever wishes to found or begin a new way, must necessarily, as the founder or beginner of the new way, precede others. Hence to the ancient people was given a certain carnal way, circumcision, in sign of future obedience and purgation; which in faithful and law-keeping persons, before I, the Son of God, the promised truth, came, operated a certain effect of future grace and promise; and when the truth came, as the law was only a shadow, it was decreed in eternity that the ancient way should depart, being now ineffectual. When, then, the truth appeared, and the shadow departed, and an easier way to heaven was shown, I, God and man, born without sin, chose to be baptized from humility, and as an example to others, and to open heaven to believers. And as a sign of this, when I was baptized, then heaven opened, and the voice of my Father was heard, and the Holy Ghost appeared in the form of a dove, and I, ' the Son of God, was manifest in true man, thát the faithful might know and believe that the Father opened heaven to the faithful baptized, the Holy Ghost is with the baptizer, the power of my humanity in the element, although the operation and will of the Father, myself, and the Holy Ghost, are but one. So when truth came, that is, when I came into the world, then immediately the shadow disappeared, the shell of the law was broken, and the kernel appeared, circumcision ceased, and baptism was confirmed in myself, whereby heaven is opened to young and old, and children of wrath become children of grace and eternal life.—Lib. v., inter. x., sol. 6.

CHAPTER XIV.

THE STATE OF THE WORLD WHEN CHRIST BEGAN TO PREACH.

THE Son of God said: Before my Incarnation this world was like a wilderness, in which was a turbid and unclean well, of which all who drank, thirsted the more, and the sore-eyed became more afflicted. By this well stood two men, one of whom crying out, said: "Drink securely, because the physician comes to take away all languor." The other said: "Drink in joy, it is vain to long for the uncertain." Moreover, seven roads led to the well, and therefore all desired it. Much doth the world resemble a desert, with wild beasts, fruitless trees, and unclean waters; because man, like a wild beast, was eager to pour out his neighbor's blood, unfruitful in works of justice, and unclean by incontinence and cupidity. In this wilderness, then, men sought the turbid well,—that is, the love of the world and its honor, which is high in pride, turbid in the care and solicitude of the flesh,—and by the seven mortal sins, had, as it were, entrance by seven ways. The two men standing by the well signified the masters of the Jews and Gentiles. For the doctors of the Jews were proud of the law which they had and did not keep, and as they were full of avarice they incited the people by word and example to seek temporal things, saying: "Live securely, for the Messias will come and restore all things." And the doctors of the Gentiles said: "Use the creatures that you see, for the world was made for us to enjoy." And when man stood so blind, as to think neither of God nor hereafter, then I, God with the Father and Holy Ghost, came into the world, and assuming humanity, said openly: "What God promised and Moses wrote, is fulfilled. Love, therefore, the things of heaven, for those of earth pass, and those of eternity will I give unto you." I showed, too, the sevenfold way whereby man might be drawn away from his vanity. For I showed poverty and obedience, I taught fasts and prayers; I sometimes fled away from men, and abode alone in prayer; I endured opprobrium, I chose toil and grief, I bore pain and contempt. In my own self did I show the way, in which my friends long walked, but now the way is broken up. The guardians sleep; those who pass delight in vanity and novelties; therefore, I rise and will not be silent. I will take away the voice of praise, and I will let my vineyard to others, who will bear fruit in season. Yet, according to the common proverb, friends are found among enemies. Therefore, will I send to my friends, words sweeter than dates, more delicious than honey, more precious than gold. Who receive and keep them, shall have that treasure which is happily forever, and faileth not, but increases in life everlasting.

Before I began to walk and labor, a voice resounded before me, saying: "The axe is laid to the tree." What was this voice but John the Baptist, who, sent before me, cried out in the desert: "The axe is laid to the tree;" as if to say: "Man is now ready, because the axe is ready." And he came, preparing the way to the city, and extirpating all obstacles. And I, coming, labored from sunrise to sunset; that is, from my incarnation to my death on the cross, I worked out man's salvation, flying in the beginning of my entrance into this wilderness, on account of the persecution of Herod, my enemy; and I suffered persecution, I ate and drank, and fulfilled all the other necessities of nature, without sin to the instruction of faith, and the manifestation of my true assumed nature.—Lib. iii., c. 15.

CHAPTER XV.

THE AGONY IN THE GARDEN.

JESUS speaks: I had three things in my death. First, Faith, when I bent my knees and prayed, knowing that the Father could deliver me from my Passion. Second, Hope, when I waited so constantly, and said: Not as I will. Third, Charity, when I said: Thy will be done. I had, too, anguish of body and the natural fear of my Passion, when the blood issued from my body. Let not my friends then tremble as if abandoned, when tribulation comes upon them; I showed them in myself, that weak flesh always shrinks from trouble. But you may ask, How did a bloody sweat issue from my body? As the blood of the sick man is dried and consumed in all his members, so my blood was consumed by the natural fear of death. Finally, my Father wishing to show the way by which heaven should be opened and excluded man enter in, out of love delivered me up to the Passion, that by accomplishing it, my body might be glorified. For in justice, my humanity could not enter glory without passion, although I might have done so by the power of my divinity.

How then do they deserve to enter into my glory, who have little faith, vain hope, and no charity? If, indeed, they had the faith of eternal joy and horrible punishment, they would desire naught but me. Did they believe that I know and see all things, and am powerful over all things, and seek judgment of all, the earth would grow vile to them, and they would be more afraid to sin before me for my fear, than before men. Had they firm hope, then their whole mind and thought would be to me. Had they divine charity, they would at least think in mind, what I did for them, how great was my labor in preaching, my pain in my Passion, my charity in death, because I preferred death to abandoning them. But their faith is weak, tottering, as it were, to fall; because they believe, when the assault of temptation is absent,—they distrust, when any thing contrary comes upon them. Their hope is vain; they hope that sin will be forgiven without justice and truth of judgment. They trust to obtain the kingdom of heaven gratis; they desire to obtain mercy untempered by justice. Their love towards me is all cold, because they are never inflamed to seek me unless compelled by tribulation. How can I be warm with such, who have neither right faith, firm hope, nor fervent love for me? So when they cry out to me and say: "Have mercy on me, O God," they do not deserve to be heard, nor to enter into my glory. As they will not follow their Lord to his passion, they shall not follow him to his glory. For no soldier can please his Lord, and, after falling, be restored to favor, unless he first humbles him to show his contempt.— Lib. i., c. 39.

CHAPTER XVI.

THE PASSION OF OUR LORD.

The Blessed Virgin speaks.

AT that time, my Son was suffering, and as Judas the traitor approached, he stooped towards him, for Judas was of low stature, giving him a kiss, saying: "Friend, wherefore hast thou come?" And immediately some seized him, others dragged him by the hair, others defiled him by spitting upon him. Then my Son spoke, saying: "I am reputed as a worm, which lies in winter as if dead, on which the passer-by spits and tramples. The Jews have this day treated me like a worm, because I was deemed most abject and unworthy by them."—Lib. iv., c. 99.

When the time of my Son's Passion arrived, his enemies seized him, striking him on his cheek and neck; and spitting upon him, they mocked him. Then, led to the pillar, he stripped himself, and himself stretched his hands to the pillar, which his enemies pitiless bound. Now, while tied there he had no clothing, but stood as he was born, and suffered the shame of his nakedness. Then his enemies rose up, for they stood on all sides, his friends having fled, and they scourged his body, pure from all spot or sin. At the first blow, I, who stood nearest, fell as if dead, and on recovering my senses, I beheld his body bruised and beaten to the very ribs, so that his ribs could be seen; and what was still more bitter, when the scourge was raised, his very flesh was furrowed by the thongs. And when my Son stood thus, all bloody, all torn, so that no soundness could be found in him, nor any spot to scourge, then one, his spirit roused within him, asked: "Will you slay him thus unjudged?" and he immediately cut his bonds. Then my Son put on his clothes, and I beheld the spot where my Son's feet stood all full of blood, and I knew my Son's course by his footprints, for wherever he went, the earth seemed stained with blood; nor did they suffer him to clothe himself, but they compelled and urged him to hasten.

Now, as my Son was led away like a robber, he wiped away the blood from his eyes. And when he was condemned, they gave him his cross to bear. When he had carried it a short way, one came up and assumed it. Meanwhile, as my Son was going to the place of his Passion, some smote him on the back, others struck him in the face. And so violently and rudely was he struck, that though I did not see the person striking, I distinctly heard the sound of the blow. And when I came with him to the place of the Passion, I there beheld all the instruments prepared for his death. And my Son himself coming thither, divested himself of his clothes, the attendants saying to each other: "These vestments are ours, nor can he have them again, that is condemned to death." Now, while my Son stood as naked as when he was born, one running up, handed him a cloth, with which, exulting inwardly, he covered him. Then his cruel executioners seized him, and stretched him on the cross. First they fixed his right hand to the beam, which was pierced for nails, and they transfixed his hand in the part where the bone was firmest. Then drawing his other hand with a rope, they affixed it in like manner to the cross. Then they crucified his right foot, and over it the left, with two nails, so that all the nerves and veins were extended and broken. This done, they fitted a crown of thorns to his head, which so acutely wounded the venerable head of my Son, that his eyes were filled, his ears stopped up, with the blood that streamed down, and his whole beard matted with the gore. And as he stood thus pierced and bloody, condoling with me as I stood mourning, he looked with blood-stained eyes to John, my kinsman, and commended me to him. At that time, I heard some saying that my Son was a robber, others that he was a liar, others that none better deserved death than my Son, and these words renewed my grief. But, as has been said, when the first nail was driven into him, horrified at the first blow, I fell as though dead, my eyes darkened, my hands trembling, my feet quivering, nor for bitterness could I look again before he was nailed fast. On rising, I beheld my Son hanging miserably, and I, his most wretched mother, filled with terror on all sides, could scarcely stand for grief. But my Son, seeing me and his friends weeping disconsolately, in a loud and tearful voice cried out to his Father, saying: "Father, why hast thou forsaken me?" Then his eyes appeared half dead, his cheeks hollow, and his countenance mournful, his mouth open and his tongue bloodstained, his body collapsed as though he had nothing within, the humors being all drained; his whole body, pale and languid from the loss and flow of blood. His hands and feet were stretched out most rigidly, drawn and shaped to the form of the cross, his beard and hair all clotted with blood. Now when my Son was thus torn and livid, his heart alone was vigorous, it being naturally very good and strong; for at his birth he assumed a most pure body of my flesh, and an excellent constitution. His skin was so tender and fair, that it could not be slightly struck without blood issuing at once. His blood was so fresh, that it could be seen in his clear skin; and as he was of an excellent temperament, life struggled with death in his pierced body. For sometimes the pain mounted from his pierced limbs and nerves to his heart, which was very vigorous and uncorrupted, and thus tortured him with incredible pain and suffering. And sometimes the pain shot from his heart to his lacerated members, and thus prolonged death with bitterness. And when my Son, surrounded with these pains, looked to his weeping friends, who would have preferred with his assistance to bear that penalty in their own persons, or to burn forever in hell, rather than see him thus tortured, this pain, from the grief of his friends, exceeded all bitterness and tribulation, which he endured either in body or in heart, because he loved them tenderly. Then in his great anguish of body, he cried in his humanity to his Father: "Father, into thy hands I commend my spirit." When I, his most afflicted mother, heard these words, all my limbs trembled in my bitter grief of heart. And as often as I thought of this word, it was present and fresh in my ears. And as death came on, when his heart was breaking from excessive pain, then all his members quivered, and his head, rising slightly, inclined. His mouth was seen to open, disclosing his tongue all covered with blood. His hands shrunk a little from the holes of the nails, and the feet bore more of the weight of the body. His fingers and arms extended in a manner, and his back was pressed back on the cross. Then some said to me: "Mary, thy Son is dead." Others said: "He is dead, but he will rise again." While all were thus speaking, one came up and drove his lance so stoutly into his one side, that it almost came out on the other; and when he drew out the lance, its point was all ruddy with blood. Then it seemed to me as if my heart was pierced, when I beheld the heart of my most beloved Son pierced through. Then he was taken down from the cross, and I received him into my bosom, like a leper, and all livid, for his eyes were dead and full of blood; his mouth cold as snow; his beard like cords; his face contracted. His hands were so stiffened, that they could not be raised above the navel. As he stood on the cross, so I held him in my arms, like a man contracted in every limb. Then they swathed him in clean linen, and I with my veil wiped his wounds and limbs, and I closed his eyes and mouth, which were open in death. Then they laid him in the sepulchre. Oh, how readily would I have laid myself there alive beside my Son, had it been his will! When all was over, John the good came and led me home. See, my daughter, what my Son endured for thee.—Lib. i., c. 10.

CHAPTER XVII.

THE PASSION.

When the Passion of my Son drew nigh, his eyes were filled with tears, and his body with sweat, through fear of the Passion, and he was soon torn from my sight; nor did I see him more, till he was brought out to be scourged. Then he was dragged to the ground, and dashed forward so cruelly, that as his head struck, his teeth were dashed together, and he was so violently beaten on the neck and cheek, that the sound of the blows reached my ears. Then at the lictor's order he stripped himself of his clothes; voluntarily clasping the pillar, he was bound tightly, and his whole body lacerated with scourges tipped with sharp points turned back, not pulling out, but ploughing up. At the first blow, as if smitten in heart, I lost all sense; and coming to, after a time, I beheld his body torn for he was all naked when he was scourged. Then one of his enemies said to the attending lictors: "Do you wish to put this man to death untried?" and saying this, he cut his bonds. And now my Son, loosed from the pillar, first turned to his clothes, but time was not given him to dress. Yet as he was hurried along, he put his arms in the sleeves. But his footprints, where he stood at the pillar, were full of blood, so that I could easily discern every step he took, by the bloody mark of the blood. Then with his tunic he wiped away the blood that streamed from his face.

When finally condemned, he was led out, bearing his cross; but on the way, another was put in his place to bear it. On reaching the place of the crucifixion, lo! the hammer and four sharp nails were ready, and at an order he laid off his clothes, binding around his loins a small linen cloth, which he to his consolation received.

Now the cross was planted, and its arms raised, so that the junction of the cross was between the shoulders, the cross affording no support to the head, and the inscription-board was fixed to the two arms rising above the head. At an order given, he turned his back to the cross, and being asked, first stretched forth his right hand, then the other hand, not reaching the other arm of the cross, was stretched. And in like manner the feet were drawn to the holes prepared for them and crossed. Parting again below the knee, they were fastened to the wood of the cross by two nails, as the hands were.

At the first blow of the hammer, I fell into an ecstasy of grief, and on recovering, I beheld my Son nailed to the cross, and I heard men saying to each other: "What did he commit, theft, rapine, or falsehood?" Others answering, that he was a liar. And then a crown of thorns was pressed tight on his head, descending to the middle of his forehead, many streams of blood flowing down his face from the points that entered, filling his hair, and eyes, and beard, so that he seemed to me nothing but blood; nor could he see me standing by the cross, except when he expelled the blood by compressing his eyelids.

After commending me to his disciples, raising his head, and lifting up his streaming eyes to heaven, he uttered a voice from the depth of his breast, saying: "My God, my God, why hast thou forsaken me?"—words that I never could forget till I came to heaven, and which he uttered more through compassion for me, than affected by his own suffering. Then the color of death came on wherever he could be seen for the blood; his cheeks clung to his jaws, his attenuated ribs could be numbered; his belly, exhausted of all its humors, collapsed on his back, and his nostrils were pinched up, as his heart was almost broken. Then his whole body quivered, and his beard sank on his breast. Then I fell lifeless to the ground. His mouth being open, as he had expired, his tongue, teeth, and the blood in his mouth could be seen by those looking on; and his half-closed eyes were turned up; and his body, now dead, hung heavily, the knees inclining to one side, the feet to the other, on the nails as on hinges. Meanwhile, some men standing by, said, as it were, exultingly: "Mary, thy Son is dead." Others of more sense said: "O lady, now the penalty of thy Son is paid to eternal glory." A short time after, his side being opened and the lance drawn out, the blood appeared on the spearhead, as it were, of a ruddy color, showing that the heart was pierced. This wound penetrated my heart, and it is wonderful that it did not burst. Others departed, but I could not.

But now I was consoled that I could touch his body taken down from the cross, and receive him to my bosom, examine his wounds, and wipe away the blood. Then my fingers closed his mouth, and I also composed his eyes; but I could not bend his stiffening arms so as to cross on his breast, but over his belly. Nor could his knees be extended, but they were bent as they had stiffened on the cross.—Lib. iv., c. 70.

CHAPTER XVIII.

THE CRUCIFIXION.

St. Bridget speaks.

WHILE I was at Mount Calvary weeping bitterly, I beheld my Lord, naked and scourged, led out by the Jews to be crucified, and diligently guarded by them. I then beheld, too, a hole cut in the mountain, and the crucifiers around, ready to perform their cruel work. But my Lord, turning to me, said to me: "Observe, that in this hollow of the rock was the foot of my cross planted, at the time of my Passion;" and I immediately saw how the cross was fixed there by the Jews, and fastened firmly in the hollow of the rock of the mountain, with wooden pegs driven in on all sides with mallets, so that the cross should stand solidly, and not fall. Now when the cross was firmly planted there, boards were set around the main piece of the cross like steps, as high up as where the feet of a crucified person would be, so that he and the crucifiers might ascend by these steps, and stand more conveniently on those boards to crucify him. And after this they ascended those steps, leading him with the greatest scoffing and insult. Joyfully ascending, like a gentle lamb led to the slaughter, when he was on those steps, he extended his arm, not forced, but voluntarily, and opening his right hand, laid it upon the cross, which his cruel torturers barbarously crucified, driving the nail through the part where the bone was most solid. Then violently drawing his left hand with a rope, they affixed it to the cross in a similar manner. Then stretching his body beyond all bounds, they fastened his joined feet to the cross with two nails, and so violently extended those glorious limbs on the cross, that all the nerves and veins were fairly broken. This done, they replaced on his head the crown of thorns, which they had taken off while affixing him to the cross, and fastened it on his most sacred head. It so wounded his venerable head, that his eyes were filled with the blood that flowed down. His ears, too, were closed, and his face and beard, as it were, covered and stained with that rosy blood.

His crucifiers and the soldiers immediately quickly removed all the boards placed up against the cross, and then the cross remained alone and lofty, and my Lord crucified upon it.

And when I beheld their cruelty, full of grief, then I beheld his most dolorous mother, as it were, trembling and half dead,—John and her sisters, who stood not far from the cross on the right, consoling her. The new pain of compassion for that most holy mother so transfixed me, that I felt as if a sharp sword of insupportable bitterness pierced my heart. At length his dolorous mother rising, as it were, lifeless in body, she looked on her Son, and stood thus supported by her sisters, overwhelmed with stupor, and, as it were, dead alive, pierced with a sword of grief.

When her Son beheld her and his friends weeping, he commended her in a mournful voice to John, and you might discern by his gesture and voice, that from compassion for his mother, his heart was pierced by the most keen dart of immense sorrow. Then his lovely and beautiful eyes took the hue of death; his mouth opened and appeared full of blood; his countenance pallid and sunken, livid and blood-stained; his body also was all livid and pallid, and very languid from the constant stream of flowing blood. The skin also, and virginal flesh of that most holy body, was so delicate and tender, that a livid welt appeared from the slightest blow. Sometimes he endeavored to stretch himself upon the cross, from the excessive bitterness of the intense and acute pain that he endured; for sometimes the pain from his members and pierced veins ascended to his heart, and tortured him cruelly with intense martyrdom, and thus his death was prolonged and dilated, with great torment and bitterness. Overcome by the excessive intensity of pain, and about to expire, he cried to his Father in a loud and mournful voice, saying: "O Father, why hast thou forsaken me?" Then his lips were pallid, and his tongue blood-stained; his belly collapsed and clinging to his back, as though he had no bowels within him. Again, then, he cried out in great grief and anguish: "Father, into thy hands I commend my spirit;" and then his head was raised a little, then sank, and he gave up the ghost.

Then his mother seeing this, trembled all over, and would have fallen to the ground in her bitter anguish, had she not been supported by the other women. At that hour, his hands shrunk a little from the place of the piercing, in consequence of the great weight of his body, and it rested almost entirely on the nail with which the feet were attached to the cross. But his fingers, and hands, and arms were more extended than before; his shoulders and back were pressed on the cross.

Finally, all the Jews standing around, mockingly cried against his mother, saying many things; for some said: "Mary, thy Son is dead." Others spoke other jeering words, and thus, while the crowd stood around, one running up with great fury, plunged a lance into his right side so powerfully, that the lance seemed about to come forth in the opposite side of the body, and when it was drawn out, a very river of blood gushed impetuously from that wound; but the lance-head and part of the handle came forth blood-stained. His mother seeing this, trembled so violently and with bitter groans, that her countenance and manner showed that her soul was then pierced with a keen sword of grief.

After this, when the crowd had departed,

his friends took down our Lord, whom his pious mother received in her holy arms, and inclined him, sitting on her knee, all wounded, torn, and livid; and then his dolorous mother wiped his whole body and wounds with her veil, and closed his eyes, kissing them, and wrapped him in a clean winding-sheet, and thus they bore him, with great wailing and grief, and laid him in the sepulchre.—Lib. vii., c. 15.

CHAPTER XIX.

THE DEATH OF OUR LORD.

The Blessed Virgin speaks.

AT the death of my Son, all things were disturbed. For the divinity which was never separated from him, not even in death, in that hour of his death, seemed to partake of his suffering, although the divinity could suffer no pain or penalty, being impassible and immutable.

My Son suffered pain in all his members, and even in his heart, which, nevertheless, being divine is immortal; his soul, also, which was immortal, suffered because it left the body. The assembled angels also seemed to be, as it were, disturbed, when they saw God in humanity suffer on earth. But how could the angels, who are immortal, be troubled? Truly, like a just man, when he sees his friend suffer any thing, from which he is to reap great glory; he rejoices, indeed, for the glory he is to gain, but grieves, nevertheless, in a manner, for his suffering. So the angels grieved, as it were, for his Passion, although they are impassible. But they rejoiced at his future glory, and the benefit to result from his Passion. The elements, too, were all troubled; the sun and moon lost their splendor, the earth quaked, the rocks were rent, the graves opened, at the death of my Son. All the Gentiles were troubled wherever they were, because there came in their hearts a certain sting of grief, although they knew not whence. The heart, too, of those who crucified him, was in tribulation in that hour, but not for their glory. The very unclean spirits were troubled in that hour, and gathered together were troubled. Those, too, who were in Abraham's bosom, were much troubled, so that they would have preferred to be in hell for eternity, rather than behold their Lord paying such a penalty. But what pain, I, who stood by my Son, a Virgin and his Mother, then suffered, no one can imagine. Therefore, my daughter, remember the Passion of my Son, fly the instability of the world, which is but as a vision, and a flower that soon fadeth.—Lib. vi., c. 11.

CHAPTER XX.

THE BURIAL OF OUR LORD.

DAUGHTER, thou shouldst think of five things: First, that all my Son's limbs were stiff and cold in death, and the blood which flowed from his wounds during his Passion, adhered coagulated on all his members. Second, that he was so bitterly and unmercifully afflicted in heart, that it did not cease to pain till the lance reached his side, and his heart divided clung to the spear. Third, think how he was taken down from the cross. The two men who took him down from the cross, set up three ladders; one reaching to his feet, another to his armpits and arms, the third to the middle of his body. The first ascended and held him by the body; the second, mounting another ladder drew out first one of the nails from one hand; then changing the ladder he took out the nail from the other. These nails extended far beyond the wood of the cross. Then he who bore the weight of the body, descending gradually and moderately as he could, the other got up the ladder reaching to the feet, and drew the nails from the feet. And when he approached the ground, one of them held the body by the head, and the other by the feet, but I, being his mother, held him by the middle. And so we three bore him to a rock which I had covered with a clean linen sheet, in which we wrapped the body, but I did not sew the winding-sheet. For I knew for certain that he would not decay in the tomb. Afterwards, Mary Magdalen and the other holy women came, and many holy angels, like specks in the sunbeam were present, paying reverence to their creator. What grief I then felt, no one can tell. For I was like a woman in childbirth, all whose limbs after delivery are tremulous, who, though she can scarcely breathe for pain, yet rejoices inwardly as much as she can, because she knows that her child is born never to return to the misery from which he came. So, though I was incomparably sad for the death of my Son, yet as my Son was to die no more, but live forever, I rejoiced in soul, and so a certain gladness was mingled with my grief. I can truly say that when my Son was buried, there were in a manner two hearts in one tomb. Is it not said : " Where thy treasure is, there is thy heart?" So my thoughts and my heart were ever in the sepulchre of my Son.—Lib. ii., c. 21.

CHAPTER XXI.

OUR LADY'S COMPASSION.

AT the death of my Son, I was like a woman having her heart pierced with five lances. For the first lance was the shameful and opprobrious nudity; because I saw my most beloved and powerful Son standing naked at the pillar, and having no clothing. The second was his accusation; for they accused him, calling him a traitor and a liar, and even an assassin, whom I knew to be just and truth-fill, offending and wishing to offend no one. The third lance to me was the crown of thorns, which so cruelly pierced his sacred head, that the blood flowed into his mouth, down his beard, and into his ears. The fourth was his piteous voice on the cross, when he cried to his Father, saying: "O Father, why hast thou forsaken me?" as though he would say: "Father, there is none to pity me but thou." The fifth lance which pierced my heart was his most cruel death. My heart was pierced with as many lances as there were veins from which his precious blood gushed; for the veins of his hands and feet were pierced, and the pain of his lacerated nerves came inconsolably to his heart, and from his heart to the nerves again, and as his heart was most excellent and strong, as being formed of the best substance, therefore life and death contended, and thus life was bitterly prolonged in pain. But as death approached, when his heart was breaking with intolerable pain, then his limbs quivered, and his head, which had sunk on his shoulders, was slightly raised. His half-closed eyes were opened midway. His mouth, too, opened, and his tongue was seen drenched in blood. His fingers and arms, which were somewhat contracted, expanded. Having given up the ghost, his head sunk on his breast, his hands sunk a little from the place of the wounds; his feet sustained the greater weight. Then my hands dried up, my eyes were darkened, and my face became corpselike. My ears heard naught, naught could my mouth utter; my feet, too, shook, and my body fell to the earth. But rising from the ground, when I beheld my Son more fearful than a leper, I gave my will entirely to him, knowing that all had been done according to his will, and that it could not have been done but by his permission, and I thanked him for all. A certain joy was blended with my sorrow, for I beheld him who never sinned, willingly, from his great charity, enduring such things for sinners. Let every one, then, in the world, consider what I was at the death of my Son, and keep it ever before his eyes.

Consider the Passion of my Son, whose members were as my members, and as my heart. For he was within me as other children in their mother's womb; but he was conceived from the fervent charity of divine Love, others from the concupiscence of the flesh. Hence, John, his cousin, says well: " The Word was made flesh, for by charity he came and abode in me; but the Word and charity formed him in me." Hence, he was to me as my heart. Hence, when he was born, I felt as though half my heart was born and went out of me. And when he suffered, I felt as though half my heart suffered, as when a body is half within and half without, when aught wounds what is without, that within feels it equally. So my heart was scourged and pierced when my Son was. I was nigher to him in his Passion, and did not leave him. I stood nearer to his cross, and as what is nearer the heart, wounds more keenly, so the pain of it was keener to me than to others. And when he looked upon me from the cross, and I on him, then tears streamed from my eyes as from veins. And when he beheld me spent with grief, he was so afflicted by my pain, that all the pain of his own wounds, was, as it were, dulled at the sight of the grief in which he beheld me. Hence, I say boldly, that his pains were mine, because his heart was mine. For as Adam and Eve sold the world for an apple, so my Son and I redeemed the world, as it were, with one heart. Think, then, how I was at the death of my Son, and you will not find it hard to leave the world. Lib. i., c. 27.

CHAPTER XXII.

THE CONSIDERATION OF THE PASSION.

THE consideration of the Passion of my Son ought to be frequently in man's thoughts; for let him consider how the Son of God, and the Son of the Virgin, who is one God with the Father and Holy Ghost, suffered; how he was led captive, and buffeted and spit upon; how he was scourged to the very inmost, so that the flesh was torn away by the lash; how with all his nerves distended and pierced, he stood dolorous on the cross; how crying out on the cross, he gave up the ghost. If he frequently fans the spark, then will he grow warm.—Lib. v., c. 20.

FRUITS OF THE PASSION.

Christ speaks.

I voluntarily gave myself up to my enemies, and my friends remained, and my mother in most bitter grief and pain. And though I saw the lance, nails, scourges, and other instruments of torture ready, I nevertheless went joyfully to my Passion. And, although my head was bedewed with blood on all sides, and even if my enemies touched my very heart, I would rather have it divided, than be deprived of thee. Thou art too ungrateful, then, if thou lovest me not for so great charity. For if my head is pierced and bowed down on the cross for thee, thy head should be inclined to humility. And because my eyes were bloody and full of tears, so thy eyes should abstain from every delightful sight. And because my ears were full of blood, and heard words of detraction against me, therefore, let thy ears be turned away from scurrilous and foolish discourse. And as my mouth was filled with a most bitter draught, and cut off from good, so let thy mouth be closed to evil and open to good. And as my hands were extended with nails, by reason of thy works, which are signified by the hands, let them be extended to the poor, and to my commandments. Let thy feet, that is, thy affections, by which thou shouldst go to me, be crucified to pleasure; that as I suffered in all my members, so let all them be ready for my service. —Lib. i., c. xi.

HOW SINNERS CRUCIFY OUR LORD.

Christ speaks.

I am God, who created all things for man's use, that they might all serve and edify man. But man abused, to his own destruction, every thing that I created for his good. And what is more, he cares less for God, and loves him less than he loves creatures. The Jews made made me undergo three kinds of torment in my Passion. First, the wood to which I was bound, scourged, and crowned. Second, the iron with which they pierced my hands and feet. Third, the draught of gall that they gave me. Then they blasphemously called me a fool, on account of the death which I freely met, and called me a liar on account of my doctrine. Such are now multiplied in the world, and few give me consolation. For they fasten me to the wood by the will of sinning; they scourge me by impatience, for not one can bear a single word for me. They crown me with the thorn of their pride, for they wish to be higher than I. They pierce my hands and feet with the iron of hardness, because they glory in sin, and harden their hearts so as not to fear me. For gall they offer me tribulation; for my Passion, to which I went joyfully, they call me a liar and a fool.—Lib. i., c. xxx.

CHAPTER XXIII.

LIFE OF THE BLESSED VIRGIN AFTER OUR LORD'S ASCENSION.

The Blessed Virgin speaks.

I LIVED a long time in the world after the Ascension of my Son; and God so willed it, that many souls, seeing my patience and life, might be converted to him, the Apostles of God and other elect confirmed. And even the natural constitution of my body required that I should live longer, that my crown might be increased. For all the time that I lived, after the Ascension of my Son, I visited the places in which he suffered and showed his wonders. So rooted, too, was his Passion in my heart, that whether I ate or worked, it was ever as if fresh in my memory. So, too, my senses were withdrawn from earthly things, because I was only inflamed, as it were, with new desires, and in turn, torn by grief. Nevertheless, I so tempered my grief and joy, that I never omitted aught of God's services. And I so dwelt among men, as not to expect nor take even aught of what is pleasing to man, except scanty food. That my Assumption was not known to many, nor proclaimed by many, God, who is my Son, so willed, that faith in his own Ascension should be first implanted in men's hearts, because the hearts of men were hard and loth to believe his Ascension; how much more would they have been so, had my Assumption been proclaimed in the very beginning of the faith. —Lib. vi., c. 61.

Some years after the Ascension of my Son, I was one day much afflicted with a longing to rejoin my Son; then I beheld a radiant angel, such as I had before seen, who said to me: "Thy Son, who is our Lord and God, sent me to announce to thee, that the time is at hand, when thou shalt come bodily to him, to receive the crown prepared for thee." "Dost thou," I replied, "know the day or hour when I shall leave the world?" The angel answered: "The friends of thy Son will come and inter thy body." Saying this, the angel disappeared, and I prepared for my departure, going, as was my wont, to all the spots where my Son had suffered; and when one day my mind was absorbed in admiring contemplation of divine charity, my soul was filled therein with such exultation, that it could not contain itself, and in that very consideration, my soul was loosed from the body. But what magnificent things my soul then beheld; with what honor the Father, Son, and Holy Ghost then honored it, and by what a host of angels it was wafted up, thou canst not conceive, nor will I tell thee, before thy soul and body are severed, although I have shown thee some of all these things in that prayer which my Son inspires thee. Those who lived with me, when I gave up the ghost, knew well, from the unusual light, that divine things then took place in me. After this, the friends of my Son, divinely sent, interred my body in the valley of Josaphat; countless angels, like specks in sunlight, attending, but malignant spirits not daring to approach. For fifteen days my body lay buried in the the earth; then, with a multitude of angels, it was assumed into heaven.

After my Son ascended to heaven, I lived in the world fifteen years,—the time from my Son's ascension to my death. And when dead, I lay in the sepulchre three days; then

I was taken up to heaven with infinite honor and joy; but my garments in which I was interred, remained in the tomb, and I was then attired in such vesture as my Son and Lord, Jesus Christ. Know, too, that there is no human body in heaven but the glorious body of my Son and mine.—Lib. vii., c. 26.

CHAPTER XXIV.

SELECT PRAYERS OF ST. BRIDGET.

I.

ALMIGHTY, everlasting God, who didst vouchsafe to be born for us of a most chaste virgin, make us, we beseech thee, serve thee with a chaste body, and please thee by an humble mind.

II.

We pray thee, O most clement Virgin Mary, queen of the world and of angels, to obtain relief for those whom the fire of purgatory tries, pardon for sinners, perseverance in good to the just, and also defend us weak brethren from menacing danger. Through, &c.

III.

O Lord, holy Father, who didst preserve intact in the tomb, the body which thou didst receive from the Virgin Mary for thy Son, and didst raise it incorrupt, preserve, we beseech thee, our bodies clean and immaculate in thy most holy service, and direct our way in this time, that when the great and terrible day of judgment comes, they may be raised to life among thy saints, and our souls eternally rejoice with thee, and deserve to be associated with thy elect.

IV.

Blessed art thou, Mary, mother of God, temple of Solomon, whose walls were golden, whose roof resplendent, whose pavement was laid with most precious stones; whose whole structure was splendid, its whole interior redolent and delightful to gaze upon. In every way art thou like to the temple of Solomon, in which the true Solomon walked and sat, unto which he brought in the ark of glory and the candlestick for light. So art thou, Blessed Virgin, the temple of that Solomon who made peace between God and man; who reconciled the guilty, who gave life to the dead, and delivered the poor from the executioner. For thy body and soul were made the temple of the Deity, wherein was the roof of divine charity, under which the Son of God, going forth from the Father to thee, dwelt joyfully with thee. The pavement of the temple was thy well-ordered life and assiduous exercise of virtues; for no grace was wanting in thee, for all in thee was stable, all humble, all devout, all perfect. The walls of the temple were square, for thou art troubled by no opprobrium, puffed up by no honor, disquieted by no impatience, seeking naught but God's love and honor. The pictures of thy temple were a constant fire of the Holy Ghost, whereby thy soul was so exalted, that there was no virtue not more ample and perfect in thee than in any other creature. God walked in his temple, when he infused into thy frame the sweetness of his visitation. He rested when the deity was associated to the humanity. Blessed, therefore, art thou O most blessed Virgin, in whom the mighty God became a little child; the ancient Lord became a puny infant; the everlasting God and invisible Creator became a visible creature. Therefore, because thou art most compassionate and most powerful, O Lady, I beg

thee to look on me and take pity on me. For
thou art the mother of Solomon; not of him
who was David's son, but of him who is the
the father of David, and the Lord of Solomon,
who built that wonderful temple, which truly
prefigured thee. For the son will hearken to
the mother, and to such and so great a mother. Obtain, then, that the infant Solomon
who slumbered in thee, watch with me, so
that no sinful delight sting me, that the contrition of my sins be permanent, love of the
world be dead within me, my patience persevering, my penance fruitful. For I have no
power for me, except one word, and that is:
"*Mary, take pity!*" for my temple is all the
contrary of thine; it is darkened with vices,
soiled with luxury, eaten by the worms of
cupidity, unstable by pride, tottering from the
vanity of worldliness.—Lib. iii., c. 29.

V.

Blessed art thou, O my God, my Creator
and Redeemer. Thou art the ransom by
which we have been redeemed from captivity,
by which we are directed to all salutary
things, by which we are associated to the
unity and trinity. If I blush for my own
sloth, yet I rejoice, that thou who didst

once die for our salvation, will die no more. For thou art truly he that was before the ages. Thou art he that has power of life and death. Thou alone art good and just. Thou alone art almighty and fearful. Blessed then be thou forever. But what shall I say of thee O blessed Mary, the whole salvation of the world? Thou art like pointing out suddenly to a friend grieving for it, a lost jewel, whereby his pain is alleviated, his joy increased, his whole mind rekindled with joy. So thou, most sweet mother, didst show to the world its God, whom men had lost, and didst bear him in time who was begotten before time, at whose birth earthly and heavenly things rejoiced. Therefore, O most sweet mother, I beg thee help me, lest the enemy rejoice over me, or prevail against me by his snares.—Lib. iv., c. 75.

CHAPTER XXV.

PRAYERS ON THE PASSION OF OUR LORD.

I.

O JESUS CHRIST, eternal sweetness of them that hope in thee, joy exceeding all joy and all desire, salvation, and love of sinners, who hast declared it to be thy delight to be with the children of men, made man for man in the end of time; remember all thy premeditation and interior grief, which thou didst endure in thy human body, at the approach of the time of thy most saving Passion, preordained in thy divine heart. Remember the sadness and the bitterness, which as thou thyself didst testify, thou didst feel in thy soul, when at the Last Supper with thy disciples thou didst give them thy Body and Blood, didst wash their feet, and sweetly consoling them, foretell thy imminent Passion. Remember all the fear, anguish, and grief, which thou didst endure in thy delicate body before the Passion of the Cross; when, after thy thrice-repeated prayer and bloody sweat, thou wast betrayed by thy disciple Judas, taken by a chosen people, ac-

cused by false witnesses, unjustly judged by three judges, condemned innocent in the chosen city, at Paschal time, in the bloom of youth, stripped of thy own clothing and clothed in the garments of another, buffeted, thy face and eyes veiled, smitten with blows, bound to the pillar, scourged, crowned with thorns, struck with a reed on the head, and torn with numberless other acts of violence. Give me, O Lord God, I beseech thee, before I die, in memory of these thy passions before the cross, a true contrition, true confession, worthy satisfaction and remission of all my sins. Amen.
Our Father. Hail Mary.

II.

O Jesus, maker of the world, whom no measure by just bounds doth compass, who inclosest the earth in thy palm, remember the most bitter grief which thou didst endure, when the Jews first fastened thy most sacred hands to the cross with dull nails, and as thou wast not agreeable to their will, added pain to pain in thy wounds by perforating thy most delicate feet, and cruelly wrenched and distended thee the length and breadth of thy cross, so that the joints of thy limbs were loosened. I beseech thee by the memory of this most sacred and bitter pain on the cross to give me thy fear and love. Amen.

Our Father. Hail Mary.

III.

O Jesus, heavenly physician, remember the languor, livor, and pain which thou didst suffer on the lofty scaffold of the cross, torn in all thy limbs, not one of which had remained in its right state, so that no pain was found like to thy pain; for from the sole of thy foot to the top of thy head, there was no soundness in thee. And yet, regardless of all pains, thou didst piously pray to thy Father for thy enemies, saying: "Father, forgive them, they know not what they do." By this mercy and in remembrance of that pain, grant that this memory of thy most bitter Passion be a full remission of all my sins. Amen.

Our Father. Hail Mary.

IV.

O Jesus, true liberty of Angels, paradise of delights, remember the grief and horror which thou didst endure, when all thy enemies surrounded thee like fierce lions, and tortured thee by buffets, spitting upon thee, tearing and other unheard-of pains. By these pains and all the contumelious words and most severe torments, whereby, O Lord Jesus Christ, all thy enemies afflicted thee, I beseech thee to free me from all my enemies, visible and invisible, and grant me to reach the perfection of eternal salvation under the shadow of thy wings. Amen.

Our Father. Hail Mary.

V.

O Jesus, mirror of eternal brightness, remember the grief which thou didst endure, when thou didst behold in the mirror of thy most serene Majesty the predestination of the elect to be saved by the merits of thy Passion, and the reprobation of the wicked, to be damned by their own demerits; and by the abyss of thy mercy, whereby thou didst then compassionate us lost and hopeless sinners, and which thou didst show the thief on the cross, saying, "This day thou shalt be with me in paradise," I beseech thee, O merciful Jesus, show mercy to me at the hour of my death. Amen.

Our Father. Hail Mary.

VI.

O Jesus, amiable king, and most desirable friend, remember the sorrow thou hadst, when thou didst hang naked and wretched on the cross, and all thy friends and acquaintances stood over against thee, and thou didst find no comforter, except alone thy beloved Mother, most faithfully standing by thee in bitterness of soul, whom thou didst commend to thy disciple, saying, "Woman, behold thy son:" I beseech thee, merciful Jesus, by the sword of grief which then pierced thy soul, to have compassion on me in all my tribulations and afflictions, bodily and spiritual, and give me comfort in time of tribulation and at the hour of my death. Amen.

Our Father. Hail Mary.

VII.

O Jesus, fountain of inexhaustible mercy, who from intense feeling didst exclaim on the cross, "I thirst," thirsting for the salvation of the human race; inflame, we beseech thee, the desires of our hearts to every perfect work, and entirely cool and extinguish in us the thirst of carnal concupiscence and the heat of worldly delight. Amen.

Our Father. Hail Mary.

VIII.

O Jesus, sweetness of hearts and great sweetness of minds, by the bitterness of the vinegar and gall which thou didst taste for us, grant me at the hour of my death worthily to receive thy Body and Blood, for the remedy and consolation of my soul. Amen.

Our Father. Hail Mary.

IX.

O Jesus, royal virtue and mental delight, remember the anguish and pain which thou didst endure, when, from the bitterness of death and the reproaches of the Jews, thou didst exclaim in a loud voice that thou wast forsaken by thy Father, saying, " My God, my God, why hast thou forsaken me?" By this anguish, I beseech thee not to forsake me in my anguish, O Lord our God. Amen.

Our Father. Hail Mary.

X.

O Jesus, Alpha and Omega, ever virtue and life, remember that for us thou didst plunge thyself, from the top of thy head to the sole of thy feet, in the water of thy Passion. By the length and breadth of thy wounds, teach me

to keep in true charity thy broad command, too much immersed in sin. Amen.
Our Father. Hail Mary.

XI.

O Jesus, most profound abyss of mercy, I beseech thee by the depth of thy wounds, which pierced the marrow of thy bones and vitals, raise me from the depth of sins in which I am plunged, and hide me in the hollow of thy wounds, from the face of thy wrath, till thy anger pass away, O Lord. Amen.
Our Father. Hail Mary.

XII.

O Jesus, mirror of truth, sign of unity, and bond of charity, remember the multitude of thy innumerable wounds wherewith thou wast wounded from the top of thy head to the sole of thy feet, and reddened with thy most sacred blood, which magnitude of pain thou didst endure on thy virginal flesh for us. O merciful Jesus, what more oughtest thou to do, and hast not done? Engrave, I beseech thee, O merciful Jesus, all thy wounds in my heart with thy most precious blood, that in them I may

read thy sorrow and death, and in thanksgiving persevere duly to the end. Amen.
Our Father. Hail Mary.

XIII.

O Jesus, most valiant Lion, immortal and unconquered King, remember the pain which thou didst endure, when all the powers of thy heart and body entirely failed thee, and inclining thy head, thou didst exclaim, "It is consummated." By that anguish and pain, remember me in the last consummation of my departure, when my soul shall be in anguish and my spirit troubled. Amen.
Our Father. Hail Mary.

XIV.

O Jesus, only-begotten Son of the most high Father, splendor and figure of his substance, remember the commendation wherewith thou didst commend thy spirit to thy Father, saying, "Into thy hands, O Lord, I commend my spirit;" and then, with lacerated body and broken heart, with a loud cry, the bowels of thy mercy exposed, didst expire to redeem us. By this precious death, I beseech thee, O King of saints, comfort me to resist the devil, the world, flesh, and blood, that

dead to the world, I may live to thee, and in the last hour of my departure receive thou my exiled, wandering spirit returning to thee. Amen.
Our Father. Hail Mary.

XV.

O Jesus, true and fruitful vine, remember the overflowing and abundant effusion of blood, which thou didst pour forth in torrents, like wine pressed from the grape, when on the press of the cross thou didst tread alone; and thy side having been opened with a lance, thou didst pour forth to us blood and water, so that not the least drop remained in thee; and at last thou wast suspended on high like a bundle of myrrh, and thy delicate flesh fainted, and the moisture of thy members dried up, and the marrow of thy bones faded. By this most bitter Passion and the effusion of thy precious blood, O pious Jesus, I pray thee, receive my soul in the agony of my death. Amen.
Our Father. Hail Mary.

O sweet Jesus, wound my heart, that tears of penitence and love may be my food night and day, and bring me entirely to thee; that my heart may ever be habitable for thee, and my conversation pleasing and acceptable to thee; and the end of my life so praiseworthy, that after the close of this life, I may deserve to praise thee with all thy Saints forever.

After five *Our Fathers* say the following prayer:

O Lord Jesus Christ, Son of the living God, receive this prayer in that most exceeding love, wherewith thou didst bear all the wounds of thy most sacred body; and remember me thy servant, and to all sinners, and all the faithful, living and dead, give mercy, grace, remission, and eternal life. Amen.

THE END.

MRS. J. SADLIER'S WORKS
Original and Translated.

We call special attention to her works, as they are admirably adapted for Premiums, Public Libraries, &c.

Alice Riordan—By Mrs. J. Sadlier. 18mo. - - - $0 38
The Blakes and Flanagans—A Tale of Irish Life in America.
By Mrs. J. Sadlier. 12mo., cloth, - - - - 75
" " cloth gilt, - - - - 1 12
The Confederate Chieftains—A Tale of the Great Irish Rebellion,
1641. By Mrs. J. Sadlier. 12mo, cloth, 684 pages, - - 1 25
" " " cloth gilt, - - - 1 75
New Lights; or, Life in Galway—By Mrs. J. Sadlier. Cloth, 50
" " " " Cloth gilt, 75
The Red Hand of Ulster—By Mrs. J. Sadlier. Cloth, - 38
Willy Burke; or, the Irish Orphan in America—By Mrs.
J. Sadlier. - - - - - - - - 25

The Cottage and Parlor Library.

The Spanish Cavaliers—A Tale of the Moorish Wars in Spain.
Translated from the French, by Mrs. J. Sadlier. 16mo, cloth, 50
" " " " cloth gilt, 75
Elinor Preston; or, Scenes at Home and Abroad—By
Mrs. J. Sadlier. 16mo, cloth, - - - - - 50
" " cloth gilt, - - - - 75
Bessy Conway; or, the Irish Girl in America—By Mrs. J.
Sadlier. 16mo, cloth, - - - - - - 50
" cloth gilt, - - - - - 75
The Lost Son; an Episode of the French Revolution—
Translated from the French. By Mrs. J. Sadlier. 16mo, cloth, 50
" " " " " cloth gilt, 75
Old and New; or, Taste versus Fashion—An Original Story.
By Mrs. J. Sadlier. 16mo, cloth, (In press.) - - 50
" " cloth gilt, " - - - 75

Works Translated from the French, by Mrs. J. Sadlier.

Orsini's Life of the Blessed Virgin Mary—From the French
By Mrs. J. Sadlier. Royal 8vo, with 16 plates, at prices from $4 00 to 12 00
De Ligney's Life of Christ and His Apostles—From the
French. By Mrs. J. Sadlier. Royal 8vo, illustrated, at prices
from - - - - - - - $4 00 to 12 00
Life of Christ; or, Jesus Revealed to Youth—Translated
by Mrs. J. Sadlier. 18mo, with plates, - - - 50
" " " gilt. - - - 75

The Orphan of Moscow—A Tale. Translated by Mrs. J. Sadlier.
18mo, cloth, - - - - - - - 50
 " cloth gilt, - - - - - - 75
The Castle of Roussillon—A Tale of the Huguenot Wars. Translated by Mrs. J. Sadlier. 18mo, - - - - 50
 " " gilt, - - - - 75
The Duty of a Christian towards God—Translated by Mrs. J. Sadlier. 16mo, half bound, - - - - 38
 " " cloth, - - - - 50
Collot's Doctrinal and Scriptural Catechism—Translated by Mrs. J. Sadlier. Half bound, - - - - 38
 " cloth, - - - - 50
Benjamin; or, the Pupil of the Christian Brothers—Translated by Mrs. J. Sadlier. Cloth, - - - - 25
 " " gilt, - - - - 38
The Knout; a Tale of Poland—Translated by Mrs. J. Sadlier. 18mo, cloth, - - - - - - 50
Cardinal Lambruschini on the Immaculate Conception—Translated by Mrs. J. Sadlier. 12mo, cloth, - - 50
 " " " gilt, - - 75
The Babbler—A Moral Drama for Boys. Translated by Mrs. J. Sadlier. Paper, - - - - - - - 15
The Gold Thimble—A Drama for Girls. Translated by Mrs. J. Sadlier. Paper, - - - - - - - 15

The Youth's Catholic Library.

The Pope's Niece, and Other Tales—Translated from the French. By Mrs. J. Sadlier. 18mo, cloth, - - 25
 " " " gilt edges and sides, - 38
 " " " fancy paper, - - 15
Idleness; or, the Double Lesson, and Other Tales—From the French. By Mrs. J. Sadlier. 18mo, cloth, - - 25
 " " " gilt edges and sides, - 38
 " " " fancy paper, - - 15
The Vendetta, and Other Tales—Translated from the French. By Mrs. J. Sadlier. 16mo, cloth, - - - 25
 " " gilt edges and sides, - - 38
 " " fancy paper, - - - 15

Other Volumes in Preparation.

Protestantism and Infidelity—By F. X. Winenger. 12mo, cloth, 75
Life of Mary Queen of Scot's—By Donald McLeod. 12mo, 430 pages, cloth, - - - - - - - 75
 " cloth gilt, - - - - - - 1 12
The Clock of the Passion—By St. Alphonsus Ligouri. cloth, 25
 " " " " gilt, 38
Revelations of St. Bridget—On the Life and Passion of Our Lord, and the Life of His Blessed Mother. With an Essay. By Rev. W. H. Nelligan, D. D, 18mo, cloth, - - - - 38

www.ingramcontent.com/pod-product-compliance
Lightning Source LLC
Chambersburg PA
CBHW030340170426
43202CB00010B/1183